lonely planet

POCKET NEW ORLEANS

Regis St Louis

Contents

Plan Your Trip 4

Top: Cajun and Creole cuisine
Bottom: Second Line Parade (p144)

Explore New Orleans ... 35

New Orleans Toolkit ... 153

FROM TOP LEFT: JULIA-BOGDANOVA/SHUTTERSTOCK, SUZANNE C. GRIM/SHUTTERSTOCK

★ Top Experiences

The Journey Begins Here

Sometimes it's the smell of jasmine that takes me back. The flower perfumes the neighborhoods in springtime, with blooms in such abundance that it is almost overwhelming. In some ways, jasmine seems the perfect embodiment of this city of unapologetic excess. New Orleans' love of food, drink and celebration is practically boundless. It's a city where fiery brass bands lay down the soundtrack not just to nightlife and Mardi Gras, but also to football games, street fests, funerals and Second Line Parades. This great lust for life is what drew me to New Orleans over a decade ago, and I couldn't imagine living anywhere else.

Regis St Louis
@regisstlouis
Regis writes about New Orleans and many other destinations. He has contributed to over 100 Lonely Planet guides.

Residential street in the French Quarter (p37)
ROBERT HARDING VIDEO/SHUTTERSTOCK

811

THE BEST

Live Music Experiences

Music plays an integral role in the nightlife of New Orleans, and the city has entire streets dedicated to performances, as well as numerous iconic places in more far-flung corners of town.

Listen to the masters weave together intoxicating rhythms in **Preservation Hall**, an atmospheric spot in the Quarter that keeps old traditions alive. (p47)

Feel the floorboards shake while watching the TBC Brass Band light up the crowd at the **Maple Leaf**. (p117; pictured left)

Hear legendary New Orleans groups like the Soul Rebels and the Radiators, along with the odd Cajun artist, at **Tipitina's**. (p118)

Walk the club-lined strip of **Frenchmen Street**, ducking into music-filled bars like **d.b.a.**, the **Spotted Cat** and **Blue Nile**. (p60)

Order a bottle of wine and watch top musicians take to the stage in the backyard enchantment of **Bacchanal**. (p64)

Drink a potent Hurricane while listening to the dueling pianos at **Pat O'Brien's** on Bourbon Street. (p50; pictured right)

Right: Bacchanal (p64)

FROM LEFT: WILLIAM A. MORGAN/SHUTTERSTOCKT, ANDRIY BLOKHIN/ SHUTTERSTOCK, KRIS DAVIDSON/LONELY PLANET

THE BEST

Eating Experiences

Food is a big part of the New Orleans experience, with down-home eateries serving up delectable perfection and vaunted dining rooms that have been going strong for over a century.

Bite into crispy, buttery perfection at **Dooky Chase**, famous for its fried chicken, gumbo and other Creole classics. (p146)

Linger over pecan-crusted Gulf fish and that 25¢ martini at **Commander's Palace**, a Garden District landmark. (p96; pictured left)

Learn how to make a fabulous gumbo and flaming bananas Foster – then feast on your handiwork at the **Southern Food & Beverage Museum**. (p97)

Feast on shrimp and grits while sipping a Bellini and enjoying delightful entertainment at the **Country Club's** drag brunch. (p65; pictured right)

Taste decadent, one-of-a-kind shrimp-and-alligator-sausage cheesecake at **Jacques-Imo's Café**. (p114)

Join oyster lovers at **Casamento's**, an old-school New Orleans institution serving up freshly shucked perfection. (p115)

Right: Cajun and Creole food

FROM LEFT: ZIMMYTWS/SHUTTERSTOCK, WILLIAM A. MORGAN/SHUTTERSTOCK, JOTAI/SHUTTERSTOCK

THE BEST

Festivals & Celebrations

New Orleans loves to celebrate, and no matter your background – young, old, rich, poor, Black, white – all come together during the festivals that pack the seasonal calendar, with Mardi Gras top of the list.

Rise before dawn and put on your costume to join the celebration on **Mardi Gras**, the most joyous day of the year. (p32)

Follow the sound of jazz, funk, gospel, blues, R&B and zydeco while bouncing between stages at the renowned **Jazz & Heritage Festival**. (p133)

Hear the roar of the crowd while watching the Saints take to the field in the **Superdome**. (p82)

Raise a frothy pint of Guinness in honor of the Irish at the big St Patrick's Day street party at **Parasol's**. (p99)

Celebrate Labor Day with a few thousand new friends at **Southern Decadence**, the city's wildest LGBTIQ+ party. (p51)

Catch one of the big fests in **Louis Armstrong Park**, like the winning food-and-music combo of **Tremé Creole Gumbo Festival**. (p146)

Jazz & Heritage Festival

ADAM MCCULLOUGH / SHUTTERSTOCK

THE BEST

History Experiences

Older than the United States, New Orleans is a trove of historic artifacts, from cobbled lanes to vintage streetcars. When exploring these places, you'll discover the people – both free and enslaved – who shaped this city.

Ride through the leafy thoroughfare of St Charles, aboard the oldest continuously operating streetcar line in the world: the **St Charles Avenue Streetcar**. (p110; pictured left)

Wander through curios from the past while learning about New Orleans history in the **Cabildo**, the former seat of power in colonial Louisiana. (p40)

Tour **Gallier House** to learn about what life was like for both the upper classes and the enslaved in the pre-Civil War era (p48).

See the tomb of voodoo practitioner Marie Laveau and Civil Rights pioneer Homer Plessy at the eerie and beautiful **St Louis Cemetery No 1**. (p142)

Browse for crafts, artwork and snacks in the covered arcade of the **French Market**, one of America's oldest public markets. (p43; pictured right)

FROM LEFT: F11PHOTO/SHUTTERSTOCK, ANDRIY BLOKHIN/SHUTTERSTOCK

WILLIAM A. MORGAN/SHUTTERSTOCK

Historic New Orleans Collection (p44)

THE BEST

Arts Experiences

The city's museums and galleries showcase works by local and international artists, and you can also see first-rate performers take to the stage at iconic venues both large and small.

Stroll your way down **Julia Street**, which is sprinkled with galleries featuring works by a wide range of local, national and international artists. (p86)

Make an art-minded journey at the **Ogden Museum**, with 18th-century portraits, bayou paintings and cutting-edge contemporary works. (p80)

See blockbuster exhibitions at the **New Orleans Museum of Art**, a pillar of the arts community in City Park. (p131)

Watch classical concerts at the **Orpheum**, a venerable arts hall that's been going strong since 1921. (p81)

Browse unique crafts and books after exploring the fascinating **Historic New Orleans Collection**. (p44)

Take a self-guided tour through **StudioBE**, a sprawling warehouse-turned-gallery space, with powerful works by 'BMike' Odums. (p63)

THE BEST

Nightlife Experiences

Great cocktails like the Sazerac were born right here, and you'll find plenty of vintage-inspired bars in which to sample them, along with backyard brewpubs, wine bars and other intriguing locales.

Watch the sky turn shades of auburn and pink while sipping a tropical cocktail at the **Hot Tin** rooftop bar. (p100)

Sip a refreshing Hazy Juicy IPA in the sprawling family-friendly taproom of **Urban South**. (p100)

See the streetcars rattle past while sipping a rosé and munching on mussels in Uptown's **Delachaise**. (p119; pictured left)

Explore the local drinking scene in the **Barmuda Triangle** in the Bywater. (p64)

See (and taste) why **Cure** ranks among New Orleans' best cocktail bars while lingering over their seasonal elixirs. (p117; pictured right)

FROM LEFT: ELLIOTT COWAND JR/SHUTTERSTOCK, KRIS DAVIDSON/LONELY PLANET

Lake Martin (p151)

THE BEST

Nature Experiences

Age-old live oak trees, winding bayous and one great big muddy river are all integral parts of the city's backdrop, and it's not hard to connect with the wilds here.

Conquer the steep steps of the Rusty Rainbow for a scenic stroll along the riverfront at **Crescent Park**. (p68)

Take a walk beside the mirror-like waters of **Audubon Park**, then have a picnic beneath the live oak trees on the lawns nearby. (p112)

Fuel up with chicory coffee and beignets from City Park's **Cafe du Monde**, then wander along the bayou amid the fecundity of the surrounding flora. (p128)

Enjoy a breezy view over the Mississippi while riding the **ferry** from the CBD to Algiers Point, a small community just across from the French Quarter. (p80)

Look for great blue herons stalking the waterline at Lake Martin with **Cajun Country Swamp Tours**. (p151)

Best for Kids

See wildlife at the **Audubon Zoo**, home to animals from near and far, including Sumatran orangutans, Caribbean flamingos and native alligators. (p113)

Roll up your sleeves for hands-on activities in the **Louisiana Children's Museum**, where you can peer through microscopes, build a levee with your hands and create music on steel drums. (p132)

Set your sights on **City Park**, with its myriad kid-friendly attractions, including an amusement park, pedal boats, mini-golf and beignets. (p128)

Watch the smiles light up as penguins torpedo through the water at the **Audubon Aquarium**. (p80)

Learn about the past through the interactive exhibitions at the **National WWII Museum**, then recharge over snacks at the old-fashioned Soda Shop. (p76)

Best for Free

Admire works by famous and lesser known artists amid the live oak trees, sloping lawns and meandering waterway of the **Sculpture Garden** in City Park. (p131)

Follow the brass band and fleet-footed suit-wearing dancers in one of the city's regular **Second Line Parades**. (p144)

Experience some of the best cultural and history-related exhibitions in town – as well as a fabulous shop – at the vast **Historic New Orleans Collection**. (p44)

Celebrate the night by taking in the sounds of live music spilling from the jazz clubs of **Frenchmen Street**, most of which don't charge admission. (p60)

Don your finest food-related-costume and join the fun at the **Red Beans and Rice Parade**, which occurs on Lundi Gras (Fat Monday). (p32)

Perfect Days

You could spend weeks exploring the wonders of New Orleans, from its neighborhoods to its vibrant music scene. If time is limited, here's the best way to plan your days.

Rusty Rainbow Bridge, Crescent Park

DAY ONE

Only Have One Day?

MORNING

Start with coffee and pastries at **Croissant d'Or** (p52; pictured). Continue to the **Historic New Orleans Collection** (p44), which has some of the Quarter's best cultural exhibitions.

AFTERNOON

Have lunch at **Dooky Chase's** (p146), a legendary spot in Tremé. Then head to the **Backstreet Cultural Museum** (p145), where you can learn about Mardi Gras Indians, the Skull and Bones gang, and other facets of New Orleans heritage.

EVENING

Have a Hurricane by the flaming fountain at **Pat O'Brien's** (p50). Continue to **Frenchmen Street** (p60), the epicenter of NOLA's live music scene. End the night with fiery jazz at the **Spotted Cat** (p60) or **d.b.a.** (p60).

DAY TWO

A Weekend Trip

MORNING

Greet the day on an easy-going streetcar ride up to **City Park** (p128). Grab beignets and chicory coffee at **Cafe du Monde** (p52), then take a stroll through the **Sydney & Walda Besthoff Sculpture Garden** (131).

AFTERNOON

Head to the **Bywater** (p57) for a bit of unstructured exploring in a boho-minded neighborhood. Peek in **Euclid Records** (p71; pictured), then clamber over the Rusty Rainbow Bridge for a wander along the river in **Crescent Park** (p128).

EVENING

Have dinner at the junkyard-chic **N7** (p70), then continue to the backyard setting of **Bacchanal** (p64), known for its wines, cheese and sharing plates, with a side of live jazz.

DAY THREE

A Short Break

MORNING

Get an eyeful of art at the **Ogden Museum** (p80), which has captivating works by Southern artists, as well as changing exhibitions. The shop has one-of-a-kind gift ideas.

AFTERNOON

Take a culinary journey to the tropics at **Carmo** (p87), then visit the galleries on **Julia Street** (p86), the epicenter of the Arts District. Later, hop onto the streetcar and head to the **Garden District** (p91; pictured).

EVENING

Have a French–Creole feast at **Clancy's** (p121), then kick things up a notch with live music at the **Maple Leaf** (p117). Alternatively head down to **Tipitina's** (p118), another Uptown classic, for more live sounds.

If You Have More Time

New Orleans' neighborhoods make a fine backdrop to urban exploring. Take a stroll amid the leafy streets of the **Garden District** (p91), then browse for new fashion, curios and gift ideas on **Magazine Street** (p98). Or make it a late afternoon foray in the arts-loving **Marigny** (p57).

Another great option for a ramble is **Audubon Park** (p112), and you can tack on a visit to nearby **Tulane University** (p116). Plus you can reach the park aboard the vintage **St Charles Avenue Streetcar** (p110), which will take you past yet more grand architecture along a lovely tree-line boulevard.

Be sure to pencil in some nature time – like a walk amid birdsong through the **Couturie Forest** (p130) in City Park or a bike ride along the **Lafitte Greenway** (p133).

Don't leave New Orleans without munching on at least one snowball. **Hansen's Sno-Bliz** (p121) whips up some of the best.

Magazine Street (p98)

RICHARD T. NOWITZ/GETTY IMAGES

A City Day Trip

Get an early start on your drive out to Cajun Country. If it's a Saturday, join the dance-loving crowds at **Buck & Johnny's** (p151) zydeco breakfast.

Otherwise, grab a coffee elsewhere in the small town of Breaux Bridge before continuing to Lake Martin for a boat trip with **Cajun Country Swamp Tours** (p151; pictured left). Most times of year, you're sure to spot alligators, turtles, snowy egrets, great blue herons and other animal life.

Have lunch in Lafayette, then spend the afternoon exploring the exhibits on Cajuns, Creoles and Native Americans at **Vermilionville** (p50).

Alternatively, focus on the region's delectable cooking by booking a **Cajun Food Tour** (p50).

On a Rainy Day

You could spend a whole day (or two) inside the **National WWII Museum** (p76; pictured right). Spread across five pavilions, the collection has many highlights, but don't miss the Road to Tokyo and the Road to Berlin exhibitions, best preceded by the evocative Beyond All Boundaries film.

Or you could spend the day with creatures great and small at the **Audubon Aquarium** (p80).

If there's a break in the rain, make a mad dash (six minutes on foot) from there to the **Riverwalk Outlets** (p84), where you can shop at outlet stores and then recharge over heavenly chargrilled oysters and tasty Gulf seafood at nearby **Drago's** (p87).

Get Prepared

BOOK AHEAD

Three months before Book hotel rooms if you're arriving during **Mardi Gras** (p32) or **Jazz Fest** (p133).

One month before Make reservations at high-end restaurants that you don't want to miss, and book tickets for plays and concerts.

One week before Check the **Gambit** *(nola.com/gambit)* and **NOLA's official tourism site** *(neworleans.com)* to see what events are on during your visit.

Manners Matter

In New Orleans, people take the time to say hello and maybe chat with a stranger. At the very least, it's polite to greet those you pass on the street and when entering a business (shop, restaurant, bar). Things move a little slower down in New Orleans, so don't lose your patience when things take longer than expected.

Essential Clothing

Dressing up New Orleanians are pretty casual about fashion, but some of the city's nicer restaurants have a jackets-only policy for men.

Rain gear Bring a light rain jacket or umbrella, since rain is always a possibility.

Sunshine Pack light, moisture-wicking fabrics and a hat to combat the intense heat and sunshine if you're visiting in the warmer months.

Things to Know

Life outside the quarter

While there's plenty to see in the French Quarter, the city has so much more to offer. If you want more of a taste of local life, be sure to explore other neighborhoods, especially the **Bywater** (p57), **Garden District** (p91) and **Uptown** (p107).

Go-cups

Drinking (alcohol) on the street in New Orleans is legal, and it's no big deal (just no glass, please). If you're not finished with your beverage or you just popped in for a roadie to take with you, ask the bartender for a (plastic) go-cup.

Safety

Robberies and pickpocketing can occur. Use common sense: don't walk around empty streets late at night, keep an eye on your bag/wallet in crowded places and don't leave your drink unattended in bars.

TIPPING

Tipping is not optional. Many service workers make minimum wage and rely on tips to survive.

18-20%+
Restaurants
of pre-tax total

18-20%
Bars
or at least $1 per drink

15-20%
Taxi & rideshare

$3-5
Hotel cleaning staff
per day

DAILY BUDGET

BUDGET: Less than $150

- Dorm bed: **$40**
- Cheap takeout meal: **$12**
- Beer at local bar: **$4-6**
- Short ride on a blue bike: **$5**
- All-day streetcar pass: **$3**

MIDRANGE: $150–300

- Guesthouse or B&B double room: **$120–200**
- Neighborhood restaurant meal for two: **$60–80**
- Cocktails: **$12-20**
- Car rental or taxi: **$40-80**

TOP END: More than $300

- Four-star double hotel room: from **$300**
- Fine dining for two, plus wine: **$200–300**
- Saints football game or premium concert ticket: **from $80**

Currency
US dollar ($)

Language
English

Time zone
US Central Time (UCT/GMT minus five hours)

TRAVELVIEW/SHUTTERSTOCK ©

TIP

The **Go City New Orleans** *(gocity.com/new-orleans; adult/child from $79/49)* pass gives free or discounted admission at over 25 sights and tours, including the **National WWII Museum**, the **Creole Queen** and **Mardi Gras World**.

When To Go

There's always lots going on in New Orleans, no matter what month you visit. Summers are blazing hot, but air-conditioning everywhere makes things bearable.

The Carnival season kicks off in early January and culminates on Mardi Gras day in February or March. By April, spring is in full bloom and it's a magical time to visit – especially toward the end of the month when Jazz Fest kicks off. The heavy heat arrives by early June, which is also the start of hurricane season. Things start to cool off by October, another great month. The end of the year brings more merriment, with Christmas and New Year's celebrations.

New Orleans' Biggest Events

February: Mardi Gras (p32) The mother of all street parties features one wild weekend of parades, costumes and merriment, plus other big celebrations during the weeks leading up to Fat Tuesday.

April: French Quarter Festival (p50) The plazas, courtyards and waterfront of the Quarter transform into one big stage (actually over a dozen distinct stages) during this big, free music festival featuring well-known local bands.

April & May: Jazz & Heritage Festival (p133) Held over two weekends, the huge fest is much more than jazz, with over a dozen different stages, big headliners (Lizzo, The Rolling Stones) and fabulous food and drink stands.

September: Southern Decadence (p51) The biggest LGBTIQ+ party of anywhere in the South brings revelers from far and wide for a weekend of fun and debauchery. If you're looking for the gay Mardi Gras, this is it!

New Orleans

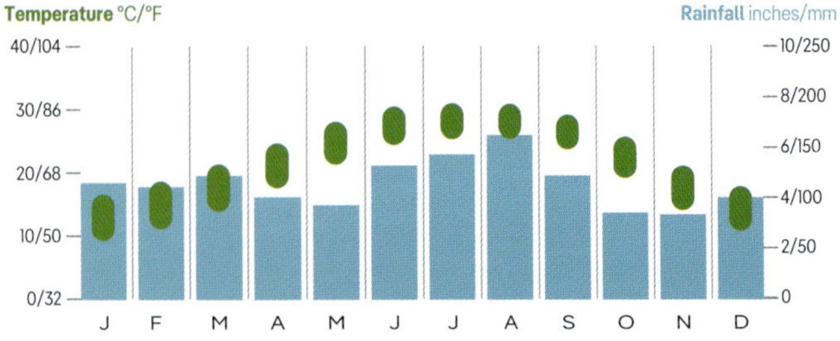

TIMOTHY GUARDERAS/SHUTTERSTOCK

Southern Decadence (p51)

Lesser-Known Celebrations

March: Tennessee Williams Literary Festival (p50) Literary panels, plays and parties celebrate the art of words. Most events happen in the French Quarter, including the 'Stella' scream competition from *A Streetcar Named Desire.*

May: Mid-City Bayou Boogaloo (p134) This laid-back gathering happens along the banks of Bayou St John, where you'll find bands and food stands, though people with kayaks, floats and canoes also hang out in the bayou itself.

July: San Fermin in Nueva Orleans (p83) Join thousands who dress in white shirts to be chased through the streets by 'bulls' – roller-derby girls with horned helmets.

November: Tremé Creole Gumbo Festival (p146) Another great free music and arts festival, this one happens in Louis Armstrong Park and features brassy rhythms, an arts market and delicious gumbo.

ACCOMMODATIONS LOWDOWN

New Orleans is peculiar in that high season falls during the shoulder months of spring and fall (February through May and September through November) and slow season falls during the summer months – meaning you can score the best deals if you you're willing to brave the heat.

Getting There

Most arrive via Louis Armstrong New Orleans International Airport (MSY). Alternatively, you can drive or take a bus or train to New Orleans, which is located at the crossroads of several major highways.

From the Airport to the City Center

Taxi

If you want to taxi into town, the airport makes the whole process quite smooth. Just head to Arrivals on Level 1 and join the line near section 7 of Baggage Claim. Rates are fixed at $36 for one or two passengers heading to the CBD or the French Quarter. It's $15 per person for three or more passengers.

Rideshare

If you're traveling as a family or in a small group, you'll save money by booking a rideshare instead. If you've booked Lyft, head out of doors 7 through 9 in Arrivals and walk to the middle curb. Your driver will pick you up here. Uber is also nearby: just take doors 9 through 11 and head to the middle curb.

Bus

The Airport Express Bus 202 ($1.25) runs roughly every 90 minutes from the airport to downtown. It stops at the Union Passenger Terminal Bay 2 and at Elk Place at Cleveland. Pick up the bus at Arrivals on Level 1, outside door 2 of Baggage Claim, zones B4 and B5.

Other Points of Entry

Bus or Train

You'll arrive by Amtrak train or Greyhound bus to the Union Passenger Terminal (UPT) on Loyola Ave, on the edge of downtown. Three Amtrak trains serve New Orleans: the City of New Orleans runs to Memphis and Chicago; the Crescent Route serves Atlanta, DC and NYC; and the Sunset Limited runs to LA. You can walk to the French Quarter from UPT, but don't do so at night, or with heavy luggage – taxis should cost around $10.

By Car

Coming from the west, you'll drive along I-10, with stretches of highway skirting wetlands, cypress trees, herons and the odd fisherman. If you're coming from the north or east, you'll likely travel along the other side of I-10.

Getting Around

New Orleans has a flat, fairly compact center, and some of its neighborhoods are ideal for exploring on foot. Streetcars and buses connect different parts of the city, and there's also a good bike-share system. Most visitors get around fine without a car, with good ride-share and taxi services coming in handy at night.

Streetcars

New Orleans has five streetcar lines. The most scenic is the St Charles Avenue line. It starts at the edge of the French Quarter on Carondelet and Canal St and runs along St Charles and out to Carrollton and Claiborne, passing through the Garden District and Uptown along the way.

Two slightly different lines follow Canal St to Mid-City. The Cemeteries line goes to City Park Ave, where it crosses the entrance to the Greenwood Cemetery. More useful for visitors is the City Park line, which heads up a spur on N Carrollton Ave, ending at the Esplanade Ave entrance to City Park.

The Riverfront Line begins at the French Market in the lower end of the French Quarter near Esplanade Ave. It loops around the Union Passenger Terminal and ends at Canal and White.

The Rampart Line connects the Union Passenger Terminal to Canal St via Rampart St, then rolls up Rampart and skirts the edge of the French Quarter before turning onto St Claude Ave.

FROM LEFT: WIRESTOCK CREATORS/SHUTTERSTOCK, SEAN PAVONE/SHUTTERSTOCK

ESSENTIAL APP

Le Pass has a trip planner, mobile payment method and real-time information for public transport.

WILLIAM A. MORGAN/SHUTTERSTOCK

Buses

Service is decent and easy to use, with some 30 different lines around the city. There are no lines through the French Quarter, though streetcars travel the riverfront and Rampart.

Taxi & Rideshares

Rideshare services are widely available in New Orleans. If you're traveling alone or at night, it's wise to get a rideshare or take a taxi. United Cabs *(504-522-9771)* is the biggest and most reliable in New Orleans. You might be able to flag a taxi in the French Quarter, though you'll more likely have to call for a pickup.

Bicycle

The city operates Blue Bikes *(bluebikesnola.com)* for rent, with kiosks across the French Quarter, Lower Garden District, Marigny, Bywater and Tremé. You need to register for a plan online or via the Blue Bikes app to use the service.

Ferry

The cheapest way to cruise the Mississippi River is aboard the Canal Street Ferry, which operates between Canal St and the West Bank community of Algiers. The ferry is open to pedestrians and cyclists (no cars).

Public Transport Essentials

The New Orleans Regional Transportation Authority *(norta.com)*, aka NORTA, oversees the city's network of buses and streetcars as well as its ferry line across the Mississippi, linking Canal St and Algiers Point.

Hours of Operation

Buses and streetcars generally run from about 6am until 11pm, though some lines keep longer hours, including the St Charles Avenue Streetcar (p25), which makes its first westbound run at 4:18am. Heading up Canal to City Park, the first streetcar departs the Caesars Casino stop at 5am.

TIP

Traffic is heaviest from 7am until 9:30am and from 3pm to 6:30pm. Allow extra time during these hours.

Ferries begin at 6:15am, with the last one at 8:30pm (10:30pm Friday and Saturday).

Buying Tickets

You have options when it comes to paying for transport. You can pay onboard, and if you don't have the exact fare, you'll be given a card with the remaining balance, which can be used toward your next ride.

You can also buy a Jazzy Pass, which gives you unlimited rides on public transportation, in increments of one day *($3)*, three days *($8)* and seven days *($15)*. Note that the one-day pass is actually 24 hours. Jazzy Passes are sold at four ticket machines in town, at various Walgreens pharmacies and at the NORTA office on Canal St. You can also buy the pass or individual rides through the Le Pass app.

Etiquette

As with public transport the world over, let passengers get off the bus or streetcar before you attempt to board. If you're waiting for the streetcar or bus, make sure you're standing near the stop, and make your presence known. Drivers bypass stops if no one is embarking or disembarking. It's polite to say 'thank you' to the driver as you disembark.

Accessibility

All buses and ferries are fully accessible. Red streetcars on the Canal St, Rampart Riverfront and Loyola–UPT lines are also accessible. Only some of the green streetcars that run along St Charles Avenue are accessible to the standards of the Americans with Disabilities Act (ADA); these run approximately once an hour. Identify these by looking for the universal accessibility icon on the front and side. Note that there are only six ADA-accessible stops, including Jackson, Louisiana and Napoleon. NORTA also offers a curb-to-curb paratransit service *(one-way $2)*, that provides alternative transportation for those who can't ride regular buses. For more information, call RTA Paratransit *(504-827-7433)*.

TRAVEL COSTS

Streetcar/bus
One-way adult/child
$1.25/50¢

Blue Bike
$1 to unlock, plus 15¢/min

Ferry
One-way adult/child $2/1

A Few Surprises

Sure, there are streetcar rides and live jazz, but you can also dial things up a notch with vampire shops, insect exhibitions and naked bike rides.

Vampire Essentials

The dungeon-esque **Boutique du Vampyre** *(feelthebite.com)*, located in the French Quarter, stocks all kinds of vampire-themed gifts. Come here for books, curses, spells, fangs, coffin boxes, bottles of blood and other souvenirs, along with witty banter from the clerks who oversee this curious crypt. Among the items for sale is a deck of tarot cards with truly surreal, somewhat disturbing artwork. There's also a mechanized doll that will tell your fortune for five bucks. Ask for the password to the Potions speakeasy around the corner if you don't mind paying a cover charge.

Running of the Bulls

Reason enough to visit in July, **San Fermin in Nueva Orleans** (p83; *nolabulls.com*) is a riotously fun event modeled on the Running of the Bulls in Pamplona. As in Spain, participants don their festive whites, replete with red sash and red neckerchief, and lace up their running shoes to run through the streets pursued by 'bulls.' Only here, the 'bulls' are horn-wearing roller-derby women wielding plastic bats, which are used to whack the bottoms of any runners they come across. The action happens early in the morning, followed by lots of drinking and celebration. Reserve tickets online.

White Linen Night

Back in the day, New Orleanians wore flowy white linen to stave off the deep summer heat. More recently, they created **White Linen Night** to resuscitate flagging tourism during the same period. Folks dress all in white and wander around the art galleries of **Julia Street** (p86), hit up the annual parties at the **Contemporary Arts Center** (p81; *cacno.org*) and knock back a small river's worth of wine and cocktails. Live bands and DJs set up at strategic points around the neighborhood, and you'll also find plenty of stalls selling food and drink. It all happens on the first Saturday of August from 5pm to 10pm – though lately, the **Ogden Museum** (p80) and the CAC have kept things going with after-parties running until midnight or 1am. These parties cost extra, but venturing into the other galleries won't cost you anything.

Boutique du Vampyre

Dirty Linen Nights (p31)

JOHN_SINCLAIR/SHUTTERSTOCK

Audubon Park (p112)

INSPIRED BY MAPS/SHUTTERSTOCK

Historic Voodoo Museum (p45)

Celebrating Dirty Linen

If you're wearing white linen – especially in a city as hot and steamy as New Orleans – your finery won't stay fine for long. **Dirty Linen Night**, thrown in the deep depths of hottest summer, is the tongue-in-cheek response to White Linen Night, and it happens a week after White Linen (ie the second Saturday in August). It primarily consists of a free gallery night along the French Quarter's Royal St. Expect lots of wine, food trucks and after-parties.

Hyams Fountain

All through the hot months, families bring their kids and/or dogs to **Hyams Fountain** to splash in inches-deep water under the shadow of oak trees and the smiling statue of benefactress Sara Lavinia Hyams. The fountain is located in **Audubon Park** (p112), between Magazine St and the outer walls of the zoo.

Realm of Insects

Embrace the earth's true overlords at the **Insectarium** in Audubon Park – there are over 1 billion insects for every human being, after all. In a separate section of the **Audubon Aquarium** (p80), you'll find a wide variety of critters, from massive Hercules beetles to the rare golden-eyed stick insect, along with a small troop of leafcutter ants. Displays are mostly geared toward younger visitors, though everyone delights in the Butterfly Garden, with striking blue morphos and numerous other species winging past.

World Naked Bike Ride

Cycling enthusiasts and exhibitionists unite in early June during **World Naked Bike Ride Day**. The credo is 'as bare as you dare,' which for some means donning nothing at all. Others opt for bikini bottoms (and/or tops), strategically placed plasters, body paint and plenty of shimmery glitter. The event unfolds on a Saturday afternoon, when several hundred underdressed riders (carefully) mount their saddles and pedal through the Bywater and the French Quarter.

OFFBEAT NEW ORLEANS

- See some of New Orleans' most talented burlesque performers at the fun and whimsical **Fleur de Tease** variety show. (p51)
- Make experimental sounds on surreal instruments at **Music Box Village**. (p63)
- Dispel the myths and get a deeper understanding of the complex syncretic religion of Voodoo at the **Historic Voodoo Museum**. (p45)
- Go for a self-guided stroll in the **Garden District**, past atmospheric mansions featured in fantastical and creepy films. (p91)
- Listen to the shuddering of the leaves and the ethereal chimes in the branches as the wind plays across the **Singing Oak in City Park**. (p130)

★ TRIP PLANNER

Mardi Gras!

Mardi Gras is about many things: massive floats rolling through packed streets, hilariously costumed krewes (parading societies) shimmying to vintage disco, vast marching bands blasting out heart-pounding rhythms, and all-day street parties. Joining in is the best way to experience the revelry.

PLANNING TIP
Download WDSU's Parade Tracker app, which shows the exact location of the krewes as they roll through the streets. Plan to get around on foot or by bicycle, as many roads will be closed.

Scan this QR code for more insights, info & special events.

Parades

The festival of Mardi Gras occurs over a 12-day period, typically in February. It begins two Fridays before Fat Tuesday (ie 'Mardi Gras'), the extravagant finale. The celebration is tied to the old Catholic calendar when celebrants would let loose, racking up a few sins before the arrival of the more sombre days of Lent. The early parades are charming, neighborly processions that whet your appetite for the size, grandeur and spectacle of the final weekend.

Donning a Costume

If you're watching one of the big float-filled parades that start in Uptown or Mid-City, don your finest purple, green and gold outfit (shops like **Fleurty Girl** on 3117 Magazine St sell eye-catching essentials). If you don't have the apparel, visit a costume shop or second-hand store upon arrival. Or you can get more creative and find something dazzling for one of the walking parades around town.

For *Star Wars* fans, dress up as your favorite character at Chewbaccus *(chewbacchus.org)*. You'll see large troupes of dancing Princess Leias, giant pink-furred wookies, alien jesters, marching robots, spinning wheels powered by human cheetahs, pedal-powered gizmos with giant light-up tentacles and plenty more surprises. On Lundi Gras (Fat Monday, the day before Mardi Gras), folks dress up in costumes made from dry beans and other local

GTS PRODUCTIONS/SHUTTERSTOCK

food items. Keep an eye out for the Beanmobile – a vintage Volkswagen featuring a legume mosaic.

For truly fantastic outfits, march with the Society of St Ann on Mardi Gras morning. Parading from the Bywater to the Mississippi, you'll spot the best costumes of Carnival season right here.

Krewes

Krewes are Mardi Gras social organizations; each krewe has a different theme and parades on a particular night. All krewes distribute 'throws' – beads, jewelry, sunglasses, frisbees and more. A few favorite krewes include Krewe du Vieux, an old-school walking parade with satirical, hilarious and downright lewd floats; and Muses, an all-female krewe known for their creative floats and throws of hand-painted, blinged-up shoes. Zulu is New Orleans' oldest, most famous African American krewe, and their painted coconuts are coveted throws.

FOOD & DRINK
Most New Orleanians stake out the parade with cold drinks and snacks. Grocery stores are a good bet for ready-made meals. You'll also find food trucks (with long lines) off the major intersections.

Explore New Orleans

Worth a Trip

New Orlean's Walking Tours

St Louis Cathedral, Jackson Square (p43)
SEAN PAVONE/SHUTTERSTOCK

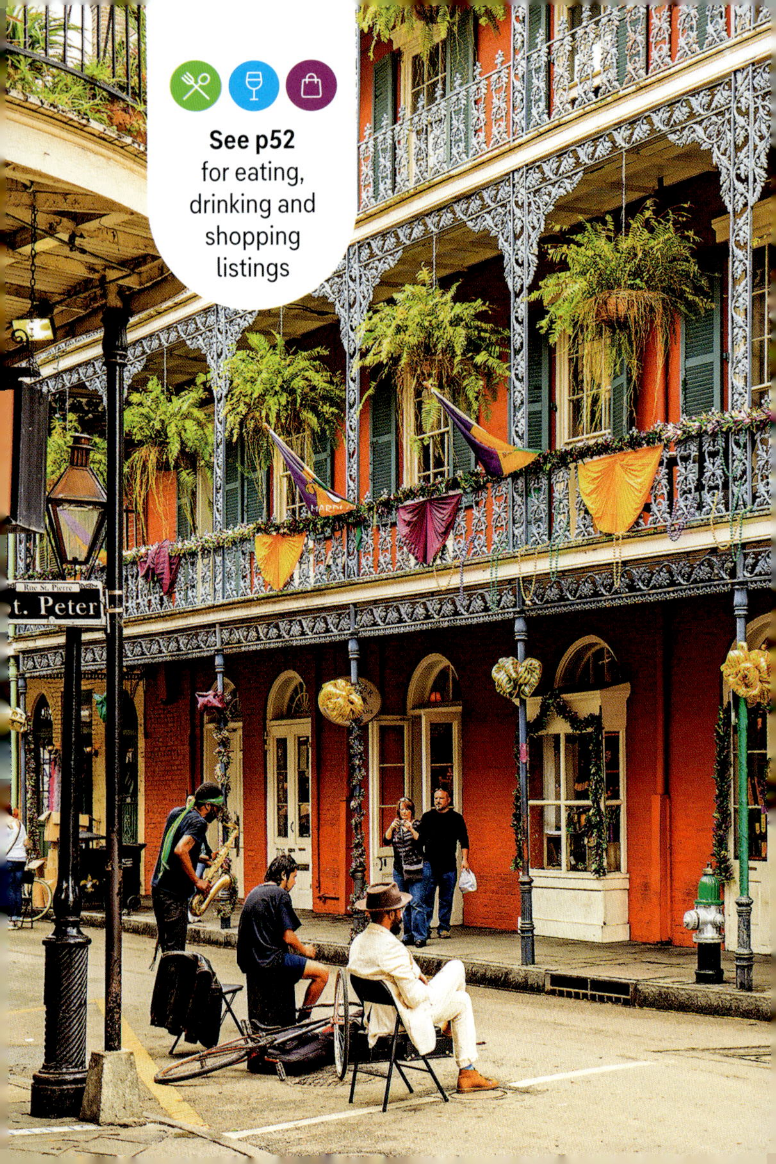

See p52 for eating, drinking and shopping listings

Explore
The French Quarter

More commonly called 'the Quarter,' this is the original city as planned by the French in the 1700s. Here lies the infamous Bourbon Street, along with the elegantly aged architecture of a bygone era, with wrought-iron balconies and hidden courtyard gardens. The attractions are many, and it's easy to see why first-time visitors to New Orleans have a hard time leaving this district. You'll find some excellent museums set in historic buildings, photogenic streets lined with antique shops and galleries, abundant options when it comes to dining and nightlife, and the serene riverfront when you need a break from the action.

Getting Around

On Foot

The French Quarter is small enough that you can walk from one end to the other in 20 minutes.

Bicycle

It's a breeze getting around by bicycle. Rent a fat-tire cruiser bike for the battered streets, and avoid Decatur and Rampart.

Streetcar

When you're ready to leave the Quarter, head to Canal St for the red line (City Park and Cemeteries), or cross Canal to Carondelet and catch the green line to Garden District and Uptown.

Jazz band on the streets of the French Quarter
GTS PRODUCTIONS/SHUTTERSTOCK

★

THE BEST

ART & CULTURE MUSEUM Historic New Orleans Collection (p44)

RIVERBOAT TRIP Steamboat Natchez (p45)

VINTAGE JAZZ EXPERIENCE Preservation Hall (p47)

HISTORIC HOUSE TOUR Gallier House (p48)

BAR ON BOURBON STREET Pat O'Brien's (p50)

A
B
C
D
1
2
3
4
5
6
Municipal Auditorium
Louis Armstrong Park
Lafitte Ave
Lafitte Greenway
St Ann St
N Rampart St
Crozat St
Basin St
Burgundy St
Dumaine St
St Ann St
Dauphine St
Fritzel's European Jazz Pub
Orleans St
St Peter St
Toulouse St
Preservation Hall
Pat O'Brien's
St Louis St
Bourbon St
MS Rau Antiques
Historic New Orleans Collection
Hermann-Grima House
Fleur de Tease
Conti St
New Orleans Pharmacy Museum
Bourbon Street
Bienville St
Dauphine St
Burgundy St
St Louis St
New Orleans School of Cooking
Iberville St
Exchange Pl
Chartres St
Bienville St
Baronne St
Canal St
Carondelet St
St Charles Ave
Canal St/Camp St/ Chartres St
Decatur St
Clinton St
N Peters St
59 72 66 65 19 11 20 38 70 33 37 9 46 14 21 43 1 48 74 28 50 2 10 68 45 47 31 75 12 44 42 61 54 41 29 22 25 52 76 71 55 30 53 67 49 60 56 58

E
F
G
H
1
2
3
4
5
6
13 Gallier House Museum
Historic BK House & Gardens 15
8 Old Ursuline Convent
7 New Orleans Jazz Museum at the Old US Mint
6 Historic Voodoo Museum
Cajun Encounters 18
Lower Pontalba Buildings
Presbytère
16 Faulkner House Books
Cabildo
17
Le Petit Théâtre
Woldenberg Park
Mississippi River
4 Steamboat Natchez
Woldenberg Park
3 Riverfront
5
Ursulines
Dumaine
Toulouse
Bienville
Esplanade Av
Barracks St
Governor Nicholls St
Ursulines Ave
St Philip St
French Market Pl
N Peters St
Chartres St
Royal St
Madison St
Pirate Al
Antoine Al
St Ann St
Decatur St
St Peter St
Wilkinson St
Moonwalk
Conti St
N Front St
32
34
64
57
26
23
63
78
36
79
77
24
35
62
27
39
40
73
51
69
For more see
Top Experiences p40
Experiences p44
Eating p52
Drinking p54
Shopping p55
0 200 m
0 0.1 miles

★ TOP EXPERIENCE

Cabildo

The former seat of power in colonial Louisiana serves as the gateway for explorations of the region's multi-layered history. The Cabildo, the Spanish term for a city council, leads visitors into airy halls reminiscent of Spanish architectural design and features a narrow, steep-sided mansard roof added in the French style.

MAP: P38 **E3**

PLANNING TIP
Although the Cabildo is closed Mondays, Friends of the Cabildo still offer daily walking tours. Take a peek at Jackson Square from the large windows on the 2nd floor.

Scan this QR code for prices and opening hours.

Journey into the Past

From Native American tools on the 1st floor to 'Wanted' posters for escaped enslaved people on the 3rd, the exhibits do a good job of reaffirming the role the building and the surrounding region have played in history. Highlights include an entire section dedicated to the Battle of New Orleans, anchored by an enormous oil painting by 19th-century French artist Eugène Louis Lami; a historical Plan de la Nouvelle Orléans from 1744, showing a four-block-deep city; and the death mask of Napoleon Bonaparte. The wing of the Cabildo dedicated to post-Civil War Reconstruction is an even-handed and thorough attempt at explaining this difficult period and its consequences. Give yourself at least two hours to explore.

Sala Capitular

The magnificent Sala Capitular (Capitol Room), a council room fronted by enormous windows with sweeping views onto Jackson Square, was the most important room in Louisiana for decades. Civic functions and legal actions were conducted here; this was the courtroom where Plessy v Ferguson, the 1896 case that legalized segregation under the 'separate but equal' doctrine, was tried. The Sala now also includes a comprehensive exhibition dedicated to the Louisiana Purchase.

★ TOP EXPERIENCE

Presbytère

Overlooking Jackson Square, the Presbytère was originally designed in 1791 as a monastic residence. That never panned out, and the building saw various uses before becoming a museum in 1911. Today's exhibitions showcase unique aspects of local life, documenting everything from fashion to art to music.

MAP: P38 **E3**

Carnival Time

The wonderful permanent exhibit on Mardi Gras exhaustively explores the city's most famous holiday. Through an encyclopedia's worth of material on the krewes (parade marching-clubs), secret societies, costumes and racial histories that are the threads of the complex Mardi Gras tapestry, you'll find that there's more to Fat Tuesday than wanton debauchery. Climb up a parade float, see some blingy costumes, watch videos and listen to the brassy, drum-pounding roar of the marching bands – the real highlight of Mardi Gras. You can almost imagine yourself waiting for throws on St Charles Ave as you duck inside one of the porta-potties (a bit of whimsy hiding a real bathroom inside) that are as rare as spun gold on Mardi Gras day.

Katrina & Beyond

The Living with Hurricanes exhibit is the best of the many spaces in New Orleans dedicated to explaining the impact of Katrina. It tackles the issue of how the city survives within the hurricane zone. Multimedia displays, stark photography, several attics' worth (literally) of found objects and a thoughtful layout combine to create a powerful multisensory experience for visitors.

PLANNING TIP

Get a 20% discount on tickets to the Louisiana State Museums (Presbytère, Cabildo, 1850 House Museum and New Orleans Jazz Museum) if you buy them at the same time.

Scan this QR code for prices and opening hours.

WALKING TOUR

Walk the Vieux Carré

Explore the historic French Quarter ('Vieux Carré') on this walk, taking in eclectic architecture, iconic monuments and a grand sweep of riverside. The experience changes depending on what time of day you go: head out in the morning to see it at its most serene, or come in the afternoon for crowds, buzzing energy, and street musicians and artists.

START	END	LENGTH
Jackson Square	Riverfront	1 mile; 1½ hours

1 America's Great Town Square

Sprinkled with lazing loungers, surrounded by fortune tellers, sketch artists and traveling performers, and overlooked by a cathedral, offices and shops plucked from a Paris-meets-the-Caribbean fantasy, Jackson Square is one of America's great town squares. It both anchors the French Quarter and is the beating heart of this corner of town. Have a peek in the elegant, gated gardens and spot the much-photographed statue of Andrew Jackson.

2 Striking Cathedral

Rising above the square is one of the country's best examples of French architecture. The triple-spire St Louis Cathedral is named for Louis IX, the French king who was sainted in 1297. Though the current building dates from the 1850s, previous iterations of the church date as far back as 1718. Head inside (admission free) to look at the striking stained-glass windows of important figures, including the cathedral's namesake.

3 Home of Tennessee Williams

Head around the corner to St Peter St and stop at 632 1/2. Peer up at the 2nd floor balcony to see where Tennessee Williams lived in 1946 and 1947. It was here that the renowned playwright penned *A Streetcar Named Desire*.

4 Prettiest Thoroughfare

Turn right and continue along the elegant Royal St, full of handsome storefronts home to art galleries and antiques stores. Be sure to stop for a photo at LaBranche House (700 Royal St), a three-story 1840s' home with elaborate cast-iron balconies adorned with hanging plants.

5 Nineteenth-Century Market

The vibrant multi-block French Market *(frenchmarket.org)* is a bustling jungle of curios, flea markets, food stalls and artist kiosks, and it's a great place to browse while munching on chargrilled corn on the cob. A trading post for centuries, the present 19th-century structure was designed by Joseph Abeilard, one of America's first African American architects.

6 The Maid of Orleans

The triangular square near the French Market is home to a glittering icon. New Orleanians have an abiding affection for Joan of Arc, manifest in this gilded, 14ft, 2700lb bronze statue that was gifted to the city by the people of France in 1964.

7 Muddy Mississippi

Cross Decatur and head up to the riverfront. From here you can stroll along the muddy Mississippi, enjoying fine views across the water. Plaques and statues along the way give insight into some of the lesser known people and events that shaped New Orleans' history.

EXPERIENCES

Delve into the Past HISTORY MUSEUM

MAP: 1 P38 **D4**

A combination of preserved buildings, museums and research centers all rolled into one, the **Historic New Orleans Collection** *(hnoc.org; admission free)* is a good introduction to the history of the city. The complex is anchored by its **Royal St** (p43) campus, which presents a series of regularly rotating exhibits. These are among the most thought-provoking in the Quarter. Recent exhibitions have explored the historical roots of mass incarceration in Louisiana, the state's critically threatened marshes, New Orleans women and the right to vote, and the city's vibrant social aid and pleasure clubs. Don't miss the French Quarter Galleries, with multimedia exhibits that touch on the region's history, from Native American settlement to 18th-century French colony to buzzing cultural hub.

Explore a Nineteenth-Century Apothecary PHARMACY MUSEUM

MAP: 2 P38 **D4**

Set in one of the country's oldest apothecaries, the **New Orleans Pharmacy Museum** *(pharmacy museum.org; adult/child $10/7)* has cabinets full of assorted elixirs once thought to be therapeutic, along with frightening hypodermic needles and bone saws in various sizes (amputation was one of the only surgical options available in the 1800s). This is also where Dr James Dupas allegedly conducted medical experiments on enslaved pregnant women. His ghost - said to be a mustached figure in a brown suit — has allegedly been spotted after closing time.

Book ahead for 45-minute guided tours *(adult/child $20/17)* that shed light on the epidemics, nefarious 'cure-alls' and primitive medical treatments (opium, leeches, mercury injections) of centuries past.

Take a Riverside Promenade DIY WALK

MAP: 3 P38 **E6**

When you need a break from the bustling streets of the Quarter, stroll over to the **Riverfront** for a heady dose of fresh air. The entire riverfront area has been landscaped with pedestrian paths, statues of forgotten civic figures, public arts projects and small green spaces such as Woldenberg Park, anchoring Canal St's south end. There are benches and grassy expanses where you can sit for a picnic and watch massive barges and container ships sail past. Early mornings or late afternoons are good times to visit, when you can enjoy the cool breezes and golden light falling over the river.

Cruise the Mississippi BOATING EXCURSION

New Orleans' current fleet of steamboats are theme-park copies of the old glories that plied the Mississippi River in Mark Twain's day. Gone are the hoop-skirted ladies, wax-mustachioed gents, round-the-clock crap games and bawdy tinkling of off-tune pianos. Instead the steamboats offer various excursions including history-themed tours, jazz brunches or dinners, and special holiday events. For an old-fashioned dose of slow travel, it's hard to match the charm of getting out on the Mississippi and watching the old paddle wheel propel you up the river and back down again. It's a relaxing pastime that the entire family can enjoy.

Two main boat companies offer cruises on the river, and they have similar offerings (see the Riverboat Cruises sidebar for our top picks). The **Steamboat Natchez** (MAP: 4 P38 **F5**; *steamboatnatchez.com*) departs from a pier near the base of Toulouse St, while the **Creole Queen** (MAP: 5 P38 **F6**; *creolequeen.com*) sails from the river end of Poydras St, behind the Four Seasons Hotel.

TOP RIVERBOAT CRUISES

Creole Queen Jazz Brunch
This 90-minute Mississippi trip runs on weekends and features live music and a good brunch (*adult/child $69/35*).

Steamboat Natchez Jazz Cruise
Beat the heat on a breezy lunchtime music cruise (*adult/child $60/30*).

Creole Queen Historic Cruise
Take an afternoon cruise to Chalmette Battlefield, where you'll go ashore to learn about the Battle of New Orleans (*adult/child $42/17*).

Steamboat Natchez Sippin' on the 'Sippi
This easygoing two-hour afternoon excursion comes with beer, wine and cocktails (*adult/child $42/20*).

Learn about Voodoo

VOODOO MUSEUM

MAP: 6 P38 **E2**

New Orleans' **Historic Voodoo Museum** *(voodoomuseum.com; adult/child $10/8)* is one of the best places in town to learn more about this often misunderstood religion. Tiny in size, the museum is just two rooms and one corridor, but there's a wealth of statues, dolls and paintings, as well as some posted placards, that shed light on the spiritual beliefs and practices of voodoo. At busy times, the museum can feel cramped, so avoid going when there are crowds milling about. To learn more about voodoo, take one of the museum's guided two-hour walking tours *($36 per person)*. Alternatively, stop in the gift shop for one-of-a-kind souvenirs, including gris-gris bags (good luck charms), herbal soap bars and jujus (magical amulets in the form of a chicken's foot).

Enter a World of Jazz JAZZ MUSEUM

MAP: 7 P38 **H1**

The Mint, a blocky Greek Revival structure, is the only building of its kind to have printed both US and Confederate currency. Today, it's home to the **New Orleans Jazz Museum** *(nolajazzmuseum.org; adult/child $8/6)*, with rotating exhibits on local jazz history and culture. It also contains the Louisiana Historical Center, an archive of manuscripts, microfiche and records related to the state.

Check the online calendar before making the trip, as the museum hosts concerts and wide-ranging events (jazz yoga on Saturdays, baby arts-play most Sunday mornings and periodic Tuesday balcony concerts).

Stroll an Old Convent HISTORIC BUILDING

MAP: 8 P38 **G2**

One of the few surviving colonial-era French buildings in New Orleans, the **Old Ursuline Convent** *(oldursulineconventmuseum.com; adult/child $8/6)* dates from 1745, and a visit here provides a unique perspective on the city's history. Stepping inside the simple exterior, you'll see stained glass windows, well-worn wooden staircases and old rooms that have served many roles over the years – as a convent for the Ursuline sisters, a schoolhouse, an archbishop's residence and a meeting place for the Louisiana State Legislature. The interior and adjoining church has statues, paintings and other Catholic displays, though it's the knowledgeable guides that help bring the past to life – from the challenges awaiting the first nuns who arrived from Rouen, France, in 1727 to the communal gatherings held to remember the deceased on All Souls' Day. Visits are by guided tour on Monday and Thursday through Saturday at 10am, 11am and 1pm.

Roam an Antique Emporium FAMOUS STORE

MAP: 9 P38 **D4**

With a massive 30,000-sq-ft showroom spread across several floors, **MS Rau Antiques** *(rauantiques.com)* ranks among New Orleans' most venerated dealers. The atmospheric space, which feels like a museum, opened back in 1912 and is now run by Bill Rau, the third-generation owner. There are plenty of treasures on display, from original paintings by Edgar Degas and René Magritte to cabinet-sized music boxes, along with striking jewelry, gilded clocks, rare tapestries and other objets d'art that span the ages. Despite the finery, the professional salespeople are warm and make everyone feel welcome – even if you're not in the market for a $30,000 ancient Roman glass funerary urn.

Rack up a Few Sins on Bourbon Street NIGHTLIFE STRIP

MAP: 10 P38 **C4**

Like Vegas and Cancun, the main stretch of **Bourbon Street** is where the great id of the repressed American psyche is let loose into a seething mass of karaoke, strip clubs and bachelorette parties. It's one of the tackiest experiences in the world, but there's never a dull moment here, and you can't come to New Orleans and not visit.

At Saint Philip St, Bourbon shifts from a Dante's Inferno-style circle of neon-lit hell into an altogether more agreeable stretch of historic houses, diners and bars, many of which cater to the LGBTIQ+ community. Great spots here include Lafitte's (p54), the oldest continuously operating gay bar in the country.

Listen to Jazz Legends LIVE MUSIC

MAP: 11 P38 **D3**

Housed in a former art gallery dating from 1803, **Preservation Hall** *(preservationhall.com; $25)* is one of New Orleans' most storied live-music venues. The resident performers, the Preservation Hall Jazz Band, are ludicrously talented and regularly tour the world – sometimes serving as the city's musical ambassadors, as was the case during the Paris Olympics in 2024.

Seeing a show at Preservation Hall is about hearing great music in an intimate setting, but it's unlike other venues in town. You must purchase tickets online before coming out. Shows run for just 45 minutes and happen several times nightly, and it's advisable to arrive early to get a good seat (it's standing room only if you arrive just before the show starts). Also note that no alcohol or snacks are served, and the bathroom is in next-door Pat O'Brien's bar (p50). Finally, this is an all-ages venue, so feel free to bring the kids.

Hone Your Creole Cooking Skills DEMOS & COURSES

MAP: 12 P38 **D5**

At the **New Orleans School of Cooking** *(neworleansschoolof*

THE BOURBON-POWERED ECONOMY

Locals love to hate on Bourbon Street – which can indeed be crass and malodorous – and yet the strip plays a vital role in the city's economy. Each year New Orleans welcomes over 18 million visitors, who spend some $9 billion during their stay. An estimated 80% of those visitors come to Bourbon Street, pumping tens of millions of dollars into the local economy. It also supports over 7000 jobs, compressed into 20 square blocks straddling both sides of the street – a job density that's nearly 100 times more productive than the rest of New Orleans.

cooking.com), you can learn how to prepare some of the city's best-known dishes in a fun, historic setting that was once a molasses warehouse. You can opt for a cooking demo and watch skilled chefs prepare three to four dishes *($42-47)* while ruminating on the city's culinary history. For something more immersive – and essential if you actually want to taste the food – book a hands-on class *($158)* where a pro chef will guide you and up to nine other classmates as you make a mouth-watering meal, followed by a big feast. Dishes featured in both the demonstration and hands-on classes might include jambalaya, gumbo (seafood or andouille chicken), barbecue shrimp and grits, crawfish étouffée and bananas Foster.

Visit an 1860s' Home HOUSE TOUR

MAP: 13 P38 **F1**

The **Gallier House Museum** *(hgghh.org; adult/child $17/14)* exemplifies a style unique to the French Quarter thanks to the innovations of famed architect James Gallier Jr, who designed the house in 1860. Guides here point out the unique features, including the double skylights and the indoor plumbing with hot and cold running water – cutting-edge technology at the time. You'll also learn about the building's residents, including the four enslaved people – Laurette, Rose, Julienne and Francois – who occupied the quarters out back. Access is by a guided tour (on the half hour five times daily; closed Tuesdays).

If you plan to visit the Hermann-Grima House, buy a two-museum ticket to save money.

Learn about Urban Enslavement HOUSE TOUR

MAP: 14 P38 **C4**

Yet another important landmark in the Quarter, the **Hermann-Grima House** *(hgghh.org; adult/child $17/14)* is a 19th-century Federal-style building with period furnishings that help bring the past to life. Knowledgeable guides do an excellent job of describing the experiences of the enslaved men, women and children in this urban setting, as well as how their lives differed from those in rural plantations. Visits are by guided tour (on the hour five times daily; closed Tuesdays).

Visit a Novelist's Former Home HOUSE TOUR

MAP: 15 P38 **F1**

Set in a quieter, oft overlooked stretch of the French Quarter, the **Historic BK House & Gardens** *(bkhouse.org; adult/child $10/5)* is an 1826 Greek Revival building that's full of period details. Visits are by 45-minute guided tour *(hourly from 10am to 3pm)*, where you'll learn about upper-class society – and the enslaved people who served it – along with more recent residents such as the novelist

Frances Parkinson Keyes. She hosted lavish parties (attended by the Duke and Duchess of Windsor and silent film stars Harold Lloyd and Mildred Davis) when she wasn't penning famous works like *Dinner at Antoine's*.

Catch a Southern Drama

LIVE THEATER

MAP: 17 P38 **E3**

Going strong since 1916, **Le Petit Théâtre** *(lepetittheatre.com; adult/student from $42/22)* is one of the oldest theater groups in the country, and the cozy 324-seat hall makes for an intimate experience. In its **Jackson Square** (p43) home, the troupe offers good repertory, with a proclivity for Southern dramas and special children's programming. The season typically runs from October through June, with five or so different shows, along with concerts and special events throughout the year – some connected to key city events like the Tennessee Williams Literary Festival (p50).

Embark on Swamp Adventures

BOAT TRIPS

MAP: 18 P38 **G2**

If you need a break from the cobbled streets, book a trip into the watery wilderness with **Cajun Encounters** *(cajunencounters.com; adult/child with transportation $65/44)*. This outfit runs two-hour boat rides through the Honey Island Swamp, located 35 miles northeast of the Quarter, and you'll have the chance to see alligators, great blue herons, bald eagles, raccoons and other wildlife as you glide beneath towering bald cypress trees dripping with Spanish moss.

For something different, you can also book a kayak tour. You can save a bit of money *(tours without transport adult/child $35/24)* if you drive to their launch site.

FAULKNER IN THE QUARTER

MAP: 16 P38 **E3**

Like many American authors, William Faulkner did a New Orleans stint, briefly renting an apartment in a townhouse on Pirate Alley in 1925. That apartment, now **Faulkner House Books**, is a business and bona fide literary attraction that's an essential stop for any bibliophile. While living in the city – which he described as a 'courtesan, not old and yet no longer young' – Faulkner worked for the *Times-Picayune*, contributed to literary magazine *Double Dealer* and consorted with local literati. It was also in New Orleans that Faulkner wrote his first novel, *Soldier's Pay*, in 1925.

Enjoy Live Jazz

MUSIC BAR

MAP: 19 P38 **D2**

One of the best places to hear live music on Bourbon Street, **Fritzel's**

European Jazz Pub *(fritzelsjazz.com)* is so small that there aren't really any bad seats. The setting leans rustic: benches and chairs so tightly packed that you'll be apologizing for disturbing people each time you get up. As elsewhere on Bourbon Street, the drinks are overpriced, but there's no cover charge to enjoy a set in one of the Quarter's oldest operating live-music pubs.

Head to Dueling Pianos ICONIC BAR

MAP: 20 P38 **D3**

Yes, it's a campy magnet for tourists, but **Pat O'Brien's** *(patobriens.com)* has a fabulous atmosphere and an intriguing history, and where else can you see copper-clad steampunk-esque dueling pianos playing different versions of 1980s Billy Joel hits? The courtyard, lit by flaming fountains, is genuinely lovely, but folks mainly pack in for their Hurricanes, a blend of rum, juice and grenadine. If the pianos get too much, you can cross the hallway and drink in the relative calm of their actual bar. The place refunds $3 of the glass cost if you return it. Otherwise, take the Hurricane glass home for a fine memory of the evening – even if you don't remember much else.

Join the Lit Fest SPRING FESTIVAL

The **Tennessee Williams Literary Festival** *(tennesseewilliams.net)* celebrates the great American playwright, who spent more than 40 years living and working in New Orleans. The five-day fest, which occurs in late March, features a wide range of events including readings, literary discussions, writing workshops (with notable New Orleans authors like Maurice Carlos Ruffin), walking tours and plays (staged by the Tennessee Williams Theatre Company). Most events happen throughout the French Quarter, including the much-loved Stella Shouting Contest – where participants give their best rendition of Stanley Kowalski's dramatic howl before a panel of judges and cheering onlookers in Jackson Square. Many events are free; others cost between $10 and $40 (special VIP passes also available).

Experience a Free Music Festival CONCERT FESTIVAL

The city's oldest neighborhood transforms into one great big stage – or rather 20-odd stages – during **French Quarter Festival** *(frenchquarterfest.org)*. Going strong for over 40 years, the event serves as a fine counterpoint to Jazz Fest, which precludes many locals from attending due to its high admission prices. FQ fest, however, is entirely free, and features all local talent playing funk, zydeco, folk, Latin, gospel, classical, and both traditional and avant-garde jazz, along with many other styles. The main stages are outdoors along the riverfront, in the Jazz

Museum (p46) of the Old Mint, in **Jackson Square** (p43) and in various courtyards around the quarter. The four-day event occurs in mid-April, with events running from 11am until 7pm or so. Go early in the day if you want to avoid the crowds.

Get Decadent LGBTIQ+ FESTIVAL

Southern Decadence *(southern decadence.com)* draws revelers from across the country and beyond on Labor Day weekend (early September). The huge LGBTIQ+ festival revolves around the top nightspots in the quarter and culminates in a big Sunday walking parade – which usually kicks off at the Golden Lantern (p54), one of the best LGBTIQ+ bars in town.

Celebrate New Orleans Pride LGBTIQ+ FESTIVAL

Pride events happen throughout the month of June, but the big weekend happens early in the month during **Pride Weekend** *(neworleanspride.org)*, which overlaps with Black Pride Weekend. Rainbow flags flutter from countless balconies, and the streets are packed with supporters during the big march (typically Saturday), which starts in the **Marigny** (p57) and rolls through the French Quarter. Other events include themed walking tours, plays and discos, plus a few family-friendly events like the Family Equality Day celebrations in Longue Vue Gardens (out near Metairie).

Get a Little Risqué BURLESQUE SHOWS

MAP: 21 P38 **D4**

If you're in the mood for something a bit titillating, we'd recommend catching the **Fleur de Tease** *(fleurdetease.com)* burlesque show. These talented performers, many of whom claim professional dance backgrounds, blend vintage vibes with a modern, in-your-face sexuality. Variety shows incorporate magicians, fire eaters, aerialists and a bit of comedy, along with plenty of burlesque. Fleur de Tease performs all over town, including a show featuring live music at the Royal Sonesta hotel on Friday nights.

Learn about Cutting-Edge Cocktails DRINK CONFERENCE

MAP: 22 P38 **A5**

One of the most important gatherings for spirits professionals takes place each year in late July during **Tales of the Cocktail** *(talesofthe cocktail.org)*. Traditionally held in the **Ritz-Carlton**, this week-long gathering features over 400 events, from tastings and discussions to author talks and guided bar-tours. Various admission options are available, including day *(from $45)* and week *(from $175)* tasting passes to more immersive seminar passes *(from $600)*.

LISTINGS

Best Places for...

See p38 for map of locations

$ Budget $$ Midrange $$$ Top End

Eating

Cafes & Breakfast Spots

Croissant d'Or $
23 F1
Located in a quiet area, with good pastries, quiches, deli sandwiches and salads. *7am-1pm Mon & Wed-Fri, til 3pm Sat & Sun*

Stanley $
24 E3
The iconic Jackson Square spot serves breakfast all day, plus oyster po'boys, gumbo and more. *8am-2:30pm Thu-Mon*

Spitfire Coffee $
25 C5
Tucked down a lane, tiny Spitfire pours some of the city's best brews; try the Mexican vanilla latte. *8:30am-2:30pm Thu-Sun*

Cafe Envie $
26 H1
This bright, spacious coffeehouse has a vintage vibe, satisfying iced and hot coffees, and breakfast and lunch fare. *7am-11pm*

Beignets & Ice Cream

Café du Monde $
27 F3
Rise early to beat the crowds at this famous snack spot, open since 1862. *7:15am-11pm*

Sweet Saint $
28 C4
First-rate ice cream made in-house, like chicory coffee and lemon curd. *1-8pm Wed-Mon*

Café Beignet $
29 C5
The shaded courtyard off Royal serves up delicious beignets, along with breakfast plates and Creole fare. *7am-6pm*

Sucré $
30 C5
The popular New Orleans brand has six locations, including two on Royal St, serving creamy gelato and airy macarons. *8am-11pm*

Casual Dining

Napoleon House $$
31 D4
A 1797 building with an atmospheric courtyard, it is a magical spot for classic Creole cooking. *11am-10pm*

Port of Call $
32 E1
This famous burger joint has been grilling up perfection since the 1960s. *11am-10pm Wed-Mon*

The Will & the Way $$
33 D3
Head to the relaxing terrace to enjoy creative small plates and good cocktails. *3pm-1am Mon-Thu, noon-1am Fri-Sun*

Bennachin $$
34 F1
This delightful West African restaurant serves *bennachin* (African jambalaya) and other favorites. *11am-7:30pm Wed-Sun*

Manolito $
35 F3
A culinary go-to for Cuban sandwiches, cheese *arepas* (stuffed corn cakes) and cocktails. *4-11pm*

Outdoor Dining

Café Amelie $$
36 E2
This hidden courtyard is a romantic spot for brunch and sandwiches. *10:30am-2:30pm & 5:30-9:30pm Thu-Sun*

Court of the Two Sisters $$$

37 D3

The back courtyard is a local favorite for a jazz brunch. *9am-3:30pm & 5:30-9:30pm*

Jewel of the South $$$

38 B3

Tucked behind a cottage, the courtyard here is as enchanting as the cuisine. *5-11pm Wed, Thur & Mon, 11:30am-11pm Fri & Sat*

Tableau $$$

39 E4

Book a table on the balcony for memorable views while indulging in haute-Creole cuisine. *11am-9pm Wed-Sun*

Fine Dining

Sylvain $$

40 E4

In a stylish carriage house, Sylvain has well-executed comfort fare. *10:30am-3pm Fri-Sun & 4-11pm daily*

Galatoire's $$$

41 B5

This revered institution is the place to dress up and indulge in crab au gratin and other Creole classics. *noon-9pm Tue-Sun*

Restaurant R'evolution $$$

42 C5

Indulge in cast-iron foie gras and find your perfect wine in the lavish 10,000-bottle cellar. *hours vary*

Antoine's $$$

43 C4

Bite into a piece of New Orleans history while supping on oysters Rockefeller. *hours vary*

GW Fins $$$

44 B5

A must for seafood lovers, expect outstanding lobster dumplings and one-of-a-kind dry-aged yellowfin tuna. *hours vary*

Arnaud's $$$

45 B4

Going strong since 1918, Arnaud's serves outstanding Creole cuisine. *5:30-9pm Tue-Sat & 10am-1:30pm Sun*

Bayona $$$

46 C4

A slow-food pioneer, Bayona is classy but unpretentious. *11:30am-1:30pm Thu-Sat & 6-8:30pm Tue-Sat*

Brennan's $$$

47 C4

Creole dining with famous dishes (Gulf fish amandine) and decadent breakfasts. *9am-9pm*

Broussard's $$$

48 B4

A century-old gem, it doles out decadence in dishes like Gulf fish topped with shrimp and crab. *hours vary*

Steaks

49 B6

Dickie Brennan's Steakhouse $$$

Expect quality chateaubriand and other cuts of steak, along with potatoes au gratin. *5-9pm Tue-Sat*

Rib Room $$$

50 D4

A draw for steak lovers for over six decades, the high-end dining room roasts melt-in-your-mouth prime rib. *7am-2pm & 5-9pm*

Doris Metropolitan $$$

51 E4

This modern steakhouse eschews old-world elegance while serving outstanding dry-aged cuts. 5-10pm *Tue-Sun*

Pelican Club $$$

52 C5

There are plenty of options here, though the tender filet mignon and Wagyu ribeye are musts for carnivores. *5-9pm Wed-Sun*

Seafood

Acme Oyster House $$

53 B5

Find fresh and chargrilled oysters, fried seafood, po'boys, gumbo and frozen cocktails. *11am-10pm*

Deanie's Seafood Restaurant $$
54 B5
Temptations run from BBQ shrimp to charbroiled oysters. *11am-9:30pm Thu-Mon, from 4pm Tue & Wed*

Drinking

Live Music

21st Amendment Bar
55 B5
A great jazz bar that rarely has a cover charge (one drink minimum). *3pm-midnight Thu-Sun, from 6pm Mon-Wed*

House of Blues
56 D6
Home to several different live music venues, this national chain stages some excellent bands – not just blues. *10am-10pm Fri-Sun, 4pm-10pm Thu*

Davenport Lounge
see 22 A5
The Davenport is inside the Ritz Carlton and offers quality jazz to a well-dressed crowd. *11am-11pm Sun-Thu, to 1am Fri-Sat*

Balcony Music Club
57 H1
This buzzing spot on Decatur St has live music daily with a wide range of acts – jazz, blues, rock and funk. *7pm-1am Wed-Sun*

Mahogany Jazz Hall
58 C6
The somewhat newish space has vintage vibes and outstanding performances from the likes of trumpeter Leroy Jones. *5pm-midnight Sun-Thu, to 1:30am Fri-Sat*

Cocktail Bars

Bar Tonique
59 C1
Walking a fine line between lounge and dive bar, this place shakes excellent cocktails in a low-lit setting. *noon-2am*

Latitude 29
60 D6
Hallowed ground for Tiki lovers, Latitude 29 serves delicious rum cocktails. *3-9pm Sun-Thu, noon-11pm Fri & Sat*

Old Absinthe House
61 B5
If you've never tried absinthe, this old-school saloon is a great entry point. *10am-2am*

Fives
62 F3
Facing Jackson Square, this gastropub has a small oval-shaped wooden bar where you can linger over imaginative drinks. *11am-10pm*

LGBTIQ+ Bars

Lafitte's
63 E2
The oldest continuously operating LGBTIQ+ bar in the US has lots of fun events, including the Sunday trash disco. *noon-2am*

Golden Lantern
64 F1
Going strong since the 1960s, it is a neighborhood icon with a laid-back crowd. *8am-2am*

Oz
65 D2
Your traditional, shirtless, drag-diva, loud-music, lots-of-dancing-boys bar. The party goes late. *6pm-4am Mon-Wed, noon-4am Thu-Sun*

Good Friends
66 D2
Has a welcoming vibe, friendly bartenders, and artwork by George Dureau. *1pm-4am*

Historic Bars

Carousel Bar
67 C5
Go early to snag a seat at the spinning carousel, a 1949 landmark inside the Hotel Monteleone. *11am-midnight*

French 75 Bar
68 B4
Dress up for this wood-and-brass classic with

premium cocktails, including the first-rate namesake. *5:30-10:30pm Tue-Sat*

Fritzel's European Jazz Pub

see 19 D2

This Bourbon Street original often has live music. *4pm-midnight Mon, noon-2am Tue-Sun*

Napoleon House

see 31 D4

Post up at the bar and try one of their signature Pimm's Cups. *11am-10pm*

Dive Bars

Molly's at the Market

69 G2

There's never a bad time to visit this easygoing watering hole, famed for its frozen Irish coffee. *10am-3am*

Toulouse Dive Bar

70 D3

Great jukebox, pool table and attentive bartenders, plus a cleverly concealed bathroom (look for the library). *noon-6am*

Chart Room

71 C5

The furniture is creaky, the crowd is chatty and the drinks are cheap. *noon-4am*

Black Penny

72 B2

An inviting spot for a drink, Black Penny has a sizable menu, with lots of beer – craft and Pabst Blue Ribbon alike. *noon-4am*

Shopping

Souvenirs

Historic New Orleans Collection

see 1 D4

A fantastic collection of arts, crafts, clothing and books. *9:30am-4:30pm Tue-Sat, 10:30am-4:30pm Sun*

Dirty Coast

73 E4

Sells eye-catching T-shirts and other gifts that shine a light on environmental and social issues. *11am-6pm Mon-Thu, 10am-6pm Fri-Sun*

Leah's Pralines

74 C4

This old candy shop specializes in praline. Buy boxes here or try it in ice cream next door at Sweet Saint. *10am-6pm Thu-Mon*

Hové Parfumeur

75 D5

Grassy vetiver, bittersweet orange blossom, spicy ginger – New Orleans has graciously lent its scents to Hové's perfumes since 1931. *10am-5pm Mon-Sat, 11am-5pm Sun*

Faulkner House Books

see 16 E3

Rare first editions and new titles in an elegant and tiny bookshop. Plenty of Faulkner titles, too. *10am-5pm*

Art

Michalopoulos Gallery

76 C5

A popular New Orleans artist creates memorable works featuring musicians, Creole cottages, and street scenes. *10am-5pm Mon-Sat, 11am-6pm Sun*

Rodrigue Studio

77 E3

See the wildly popular *Blue Dog* paintings at the gallery of the late Cajun artist George Rodrigue. *11am-5pm Mon-Sat, noon-5pm Sun*

Harouni Gallery

78 E2

A native of Iran but a New Orleans resident for decades, David Harouni creates paintings with a surreal, eerie beauty. *11am-5pm*

Gallery Burguieres

79 E3

Ally Burguieres' animal-centric artwork is full of whimsy and beauty, with scenes featuring Louisiana backdrops. *10am-5pm*

See p69
for eating, drinking and shopping listings

Explore
The Marigny & Bywater

Cross Esplanade Ave to enter New Orleans' first suburb, the Marigny and the Bywater. Frenchmen Street – the city's best concentration of live music bars – is obligatory no matter how long you're visiting. Continue along streets such as Burgundy, Royal and Dauphine, and you'll see these artsy neighborhoods come to life with creatively decorated houses and marvelous murals around every corner.

The businesses here are layered, like onions. From the outside they look like houses, but they also may be a bar, food pop-up, backyard jazz venue, gallery, salon or plant shop. Keep peeling back the layers, and the Marigny and Bywater might just become your favorite NOLA neighborhood.

Getting Around

On Foot
Exploring on foot – and being open to spontaneity – is the best way to experience this creative neighborhood.

Bicycle
You're never more than 20 minutes by bike from the edge of the French Quarter or the borders of Bywater. Rent one via New Orleans' excellent electric-bike app, Blue Bikes Nola.

Rideshare
Stayed out late in the Barmuda Triangle? Call a rideshare – it's just a short drive back to the French Quarter.

THE BEST

LIVE MUSIC Frenchmen Street (p60)

SONIC PLAYGROUND Music Box Village (p63)

ART GALLERY StudioBE (p63)

BACKYARD SIPPING & DINING Bacchanal (p64)

GREEN SPACE Crescent Park (p68)

Jamnola, NOLA Culture (p62)
ASOLETTI/JAMNOLA

A
B
C
D
1
2
3
4
5
6
N Galvez St
N Johnson St
N Prieur St
N Roman St
Marigny St
Mandeville St
Spain St
Music St
ST ROCH
N Derbigny St
N Claiborne Ave
Franklin Ave
N Robertson St
Elysian Fields Ave
St Anthony Ave
Pauger St
Touro St
Frenchmen St
St Roch Ave
Music St
Arts St
N Villere St
Spain St
Urquhart St
Mudlark Theater 5
St Ferdinand St
Marais St
Elysian Fields
Siberia 17
No Dice Lounge 16
42
57
59
54
St Claude Ave
Joseph Guillaume Pl
61
AllWays Lounge 11
50
25
34
35
Healing Center
21
Farrington-Smith Gallery
N Rampart St
23
Bywater Museum of Unnatural History
41
MARIGNY
44
12
Phoenix Bar
49
Port St
4
Burgundy St
Frenchmen St
31
Marigny St
Marigny Opera House 4
Kerlerec St
37
Dauphine St
Washington Sq Park
Mandeville St
Big Daddy's Bar 13
51
Homer Plessy Way
Royal St
StudioBE 1
Dauphine St
Esplanade Ave
55
Frenchmen Street
24
Little Wing & Co.
Chartres St
Franklin Ave
46
Decatur St
56
N Peters St
Governor Nicholls St
French Market
N Peters St
FRENCH QUARTER
Chartres St
Mississippi River

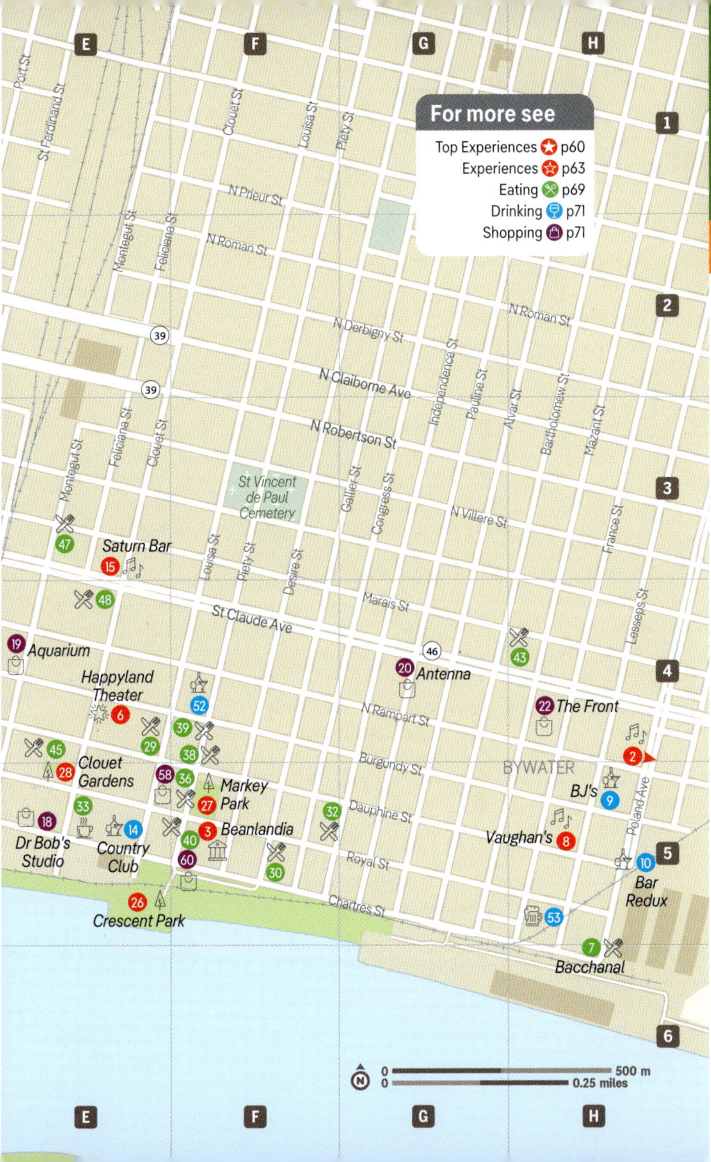
For more see
Top Experiences p60
Experiences p63
Eating p69
Drinking p71
Shopping p71
E
F
G
H
1
2
3
4
5
6
Port St
St Ferdinand St
Clouet St
Louisa St
Piety St
N Prieur St
N Roman St
Montegut St
Feliciana St
N Derbigny St
N Claiborne Ave
N Robertson St
Independence St
Pauline St
Alvar St
Bartholomew St
Mazant St
St Vincent de Paul Cemetery
Callier St
Congress St
N Villere St
France St
Desire St
Marais St
St Claude Ave
Lesseps St
N Rampart St
Burgundy St
Dauphine St
Royal St
Chartres St
Poland Ave
BYWATER
Saturn Bar
Aquarium
Happyland Theater
Clouet Gardens
Markey Park
Beanlandia
Dr Bob's Studio
Country Club
Crescent Park
Antenna
The Front
BJ's
Vaughan's
Bar Redux
Bacchanal
0 500 m
0 0.25 miles

★ TOP EXPERIENCE

Frenchmen Street

Sometimes called the locals' Bourbon Street, Frenchmen Street packs a crowd every night, but that doesn't mean you won't have a great time. Lined with music venues, street jazz and sometimes a piano on wheels, Frenchmen is a chaotic cacophony – and loads of fun.

MAP P58 **B5**

PLANNING TIP
There are a couple of 24-hour bars around, including **Checkpoint Charlie** (p71). It used to be a laundromat and now it's a bar that gives late-night haircuts on Mondays.

Scan this QR code for more insights & info.

Jazz Party

The first live-music venue opened on Frenchmen in 1976 as a way to handle the overflow from the French Quarter. More venues soon opened up, and Frenchmen quickly became the place to be for local musicians and insiders. While the street is no longer as underground as it once was, it's still a lot of fun.

Follow your ears to whatever venue tickles your fancy. There isn't just jazz, but also hip-hop, rock, bossa nova and inevitably someone singing Amy Winehouse's version of 'Valerie.' A who's who of legendary jazz musicians frequently play here, including Kermit Ruffins, John Boutté and Jon Batiste. Top ticketed events are usually held at **Snug Harbor** *(snugjazz.com; No 626)*, which dates back to the early 1980s, and **d.b.a.** *(dbaneworleans.com; No 618)*, a project co-owned by several venues on the strip. The **Spotted Cat** *(spottedcatmusicclub.com; No 623)*, **Blue Nile** *(bluenilelive.com; No 532)* and **Cafe Negril** *(cafenegrilnola.com; No 606)* – all of which appeared in HBO's Treme – are also amazing venues and tend to have a cheaper cover charge.

Shopping

Take a break from the music to pick up an unforgettable conversation piece at the **Art Garden** *(artgardennola.com; No 613)* night market. Open

ANDRIY BLOKHIN/SHUTTERSTOCK

from 7pm to midnight from Thursdays to Sundays, the Art Garden has one of the best collections of local art and handicrafts, including psychedelic prints, delicate jewelry and so much more. **Frenchmen Art & Books** *(frenchmenartandbooks.com; No 600)* opened in 1978 as one of the first queer bookstores in the South. It has a great collection of local history books and stays open to 10 or 11pm if you want to pop in between drinks. Not much happens on Frenchmen earlier in the day, but if you're around, check out **Louisiana Music Factory** *(louisianamusicfactory.com; No 421)*. It has an awesome selection of new and used records and CDs from New Orleans greats, as well as some local art.

TAKE A BREAK
If you want to grab a bite before hitting the action on Frenchmen, the stylish **Elysian Bar** (p71) on Burgundy Street has small plates and hearty dishes.

Food

Frenchmen is known more for music than food, but you can combine the two with brunch or

SHOTGUN HOUSES

Near Frenchmen Street, you'll find plenty of single or double shotgun houses, a style that originated in New Orleans in the 1840s. Shotgun houses are narrow in width and long in length, without any hallways. Some say the name originates from the ability to fire a bullet or cartridge through the front door and out the back door without hitting anything.

dinner shows. **Maison** *(maisonfrenchmen.com; No 508)* has lively jazz brunches (reserve in advance) that feature swing dancers and jazz dinners. **Three Muses** *(3musesnola.com; No 536)* puts on female-fronted jazz shows and has a small but tasty menu of local favorites like po'boys and Korean bowls – an ode to one of the bar's owners. If you're looking for a greasy snack to absorb the booze, **Dat Dog** *(datdog.com; No 601)* serves loaded hot dogs (including ones made with alligator meat) in addition to drinks. **Ayu Bakehouse** *(ayubakehouse.com; No 801)* up the street is a terrific woman-owned bakery that does interesting takes on New Orleans cuisine – try the muffaletta breadsticks.

NOLA Culture

In a fresh new location as of January 2025, **Jamnola** *(jamnola.com; $30)* is a labyrinth of exhibits created by dozens of local artists and showcases everything that comprises New Orleans culture. Reserve a time a slot online and have local storytellers guide you through the exhibits, which touch on quintessential Louisiana traditions like crawfish boils and Mardi Gras Indians. If you've been to New Orleans before, it won't be anything you haven't heard, but it's still a worthwhile indoor activity.

Local Intel

If you want to know about the fine happenings around the Marigny, or you're just looking for a friendly face, pop into **Three Muses**. Outside of its jazz dinners, the bar is a quiet refuge, and its three female owners love to provide advice to visitors. Ask about Mardi Gras mask-making workshops from October to April.

Discover Revolutionary Art in the Bywater STUDIO & GALLERY

MAP: 1 P58 D4

Eight years after Hurricane Katrina, New Orleans native Brandan 'BMike' Odums and a community of creatives transformed an abandoned, decaying housing project in the 9th Ward into an art gallery called #ProjectBE. Their spray cans breathed life into a devastated area of New Orleans, until the city demolished the buildings.

BMike expanded the project in 2016, turning it into **StudioBE** *(studiobenola.com; $15)*, a gallery where his revolutionary murals are displayed. Located in Bywater's warehouses, self-guided tours of the gallery pack an emotional punch, calling out persistant racism while sending empowering messages of hope for the future. Some of the pieces are made by local youths with the support of StudioBE's charity, Eternal Seeds *(eternalseeds.com)*.

Make Experimental Sounds SONIC PLAYGROUND

MAP: 2 P58 H4

On the edge of the Bywater is one of the most unique concert venues on the planet. Created by a group of local artists and tinkerers, **Music Box Village** *(musicboxvillage.com, adult/child$15/7)* is not just a place to play music – the venue itself can be played. Made from recycled metal, pipes and wood, the village looks like something from a Mad Max film, and everything makes noise. Come ding, dong, spin, whizz and slap the village to make your own music, or see a live performance where musicians collaborate to make a truly unforgettable sonic experience. There are usually live performances on Friday nights and Saturday afternoons. Also look out for music workshops like djembe drumming and instrument-making, as well as food pop-ups.

Catch a Carnival Krewe MARDI GRAS PARADES

Ask a local about their favorite carnival parade, and they'll probably name one in the Marigny and Bywater. Parades in these neighborhoods, usually held before Mardi Gras, showcase the city's remarkable creativity.

On Lundi Gras Monday, the **Krewe of Red Beans** and its sub-krewes **Mung Beans** and **Queer Beans** attract 15,000 people to their parades in three locations: the Marigny, Bywater and Bayou St John. Krewes are parade marching-clubs, and their members wear beautiful costumes decorated with – you guessed it – beans, an inspiration from founder Devin De Wulf's year abroad in Brazil. Visit **Beanlandia** (MAP: 3 P58 F5; *kreweofredbeans.org; adults/residents $20/15*) to admire some of the best outfits from previous

BEST PERFORMANCE SPACES

AllWays Lounge
see 11 P58 B3
Known for its sexy and hilarious burlesque shows, as well as a full calendar of stand-up comedy, drag and dance classes.

Marigny Opera House
MAP: 4 P58 D4
'Church of the Arts' for dance, theater and concerts, held inside the two-towered Holy Trinity Catholic Church.

Mudlark Theater
MAP: 5 P58 D3
All kinds of independent and fringe performances, but best known for its in-house puppet company.

Café Istanbul
see 25 P58 C3
Popular for small events like slam poetry, live storytelling, concerts and more. Find it inside the Healing Center.

Happyland Theater
MAP: 6 P58 E4
A 1914 neighborhood cinema reborn into a performing arts venue.

years and see krewe members make their costumes ahead of the parades.

The hilariously raunchy **Krewe du Vieux** *(kreweduvieux.org)* skewers local and federal politicians along with Louisiana's notorious prudishness. Intergalactic **Krewe of Chewbacchus** *(chewbacchus.org)* and its 100+ sub-krewes are another carnival-season must – they parade in all that's nerdy, from UFO floats to Goku to Princess Leia.

Join the Backyard Party

WINE, FOOD & MUSIC

MAP: 7 P58 H6
Bacchanal *(bacchanalwine.com)* is an unforgettable experience you won't find in any other city. Walk in the unassuming entrance into an impressive wine bar with fine cheeses. Grab what you like for a platter of pickles, jams and toast, and then head to the backyard to see a live jazz band playing. You can order larger bites like bacon-wrapped dates, gambas and chicken confit from the table, and there's a cocktail bar with wine by the glass upstairs.

Sip Through the Barmuda Triangle

BAR HOPPING

Quiet by day, the eastern edge of the Bywater wakes up at night with some of the city's best neighborhood watering-holes. After checking out Bacchanal, venture into the so-called Barmuda Triangle for a booze-soaked collection of beloved neighborhood dives. **Vaughan's** (MAP: 8 P58 H5; *@vaughanslounge nola*), first opened in 1959, has a fun vibe with Mardi Gras colors and Mexican papeles picados flags overhead. The Glow Worm Trio, an Italian string band that plays waltzes, polkas and the like, plays every Wednesday, and Thursdays are for funk and red beans.

BJ's (MAP: 9 P58 **H5**; *@bjslounge*) fashions itself as the neighborhood living-room; it has a full calendar of live music, highlighted by monthly shows from blues legend Little Freddy King (he's painted on the mural outside).

Enter below the neon 'Bar' sign to **Bar Redux** (MAP: 10 P58 **H5**; *@barreduxnola*), another dive bar with live music in the garden, plus finger-lickin-good Creole fried wings and gumbo.

Partake in LGBTIQ+ Fun

BARS & BRUNCHES

New Orleans has long been a refuge for those who don't fit heteronormative boxes, and the Marigny and Bywater are definitely places where everyone's welcome. Woman-owned **AllWays Lounge** (MAP: 11 P58 **B3**; *theallwayslounge.net*) hosts a nightly lineup of amazing burlesque, drag, striptease and dance lessons. If you were to pick just one event, choose the Van Ella Bordella Burlesque, which is somehow sexy, hilarious and informative all at the same time, as it shares the history of Storyville, New Orleans' former red-light district.

The Marigny and Bywater are also home to a number of gay bars, including **Phoenix Bar** (MAP: 12 P58 **B4**; *phoenixbarnola.com*), a gay dive-bar that caters to leather-clad gay men 24 hours a day, 365 days a year; and **Big Daddy's** (MAP: 13 P58 **C4**), a popular neighborhood spot where everyone can have a drink and shoot some pool.

Tour with Ghostly Figures

WALKING TOUR

Wait – was that a gay ghost walking by? Marcus Shacknow leads Walking with the **Gay Ghosts of New Orleans** *(@ms.marcusaustin__)*, neighborhood tours that tell the stories of historic LGTBIQ+ folk who wandered these streets. It only runs during festivals like Southern Decadence, Mardi Gras and Halloween.

Enjoy a Drag Brunch

FOOD & ENTERTAINMENT

MAP: 14 P58 **E5**

Located in a gorgeous Bywater estate, the weekend drag brunches at the **Country Club** *(thecountryclubneworleans.com)* have been a popular mainstay for over a decade. Seats sell out weeks ahead, but there might still be space at the bar, even if it's sold out online. There are admittedly better drag brunches out there, but the big benefit of the Country Club is that you can stick around to relax in its salt-water pool and sauna *(day pass $20)*.

Listen to Live Music on St Claude

BAR HOPPING

Many come to New Orleans for the jazz but stay for all the other music the city has to offer. St

Claude Ave is where you'll find plenty of venues hosting all sorts of genres. **Saturn Bar** (MAP: 15 P58 **E3**; *thesaturnbar.com*) is a small but mighty dive bar with live music of all kinds, from disco to funk to soul. A near-monthly highlight is the Mod Dance Party, where everyone dresses like it's the 1950s and bops together like a big blob in the tightly packed venue.

Another St Claude favorite is **No Dice Lounge** (MAP: 16 P58 **B3**; *@nodicenola*), formerly Hi Ho Lounge, it hosts hip-hop, punk, bluegrass, Americana and New Orleans brass. If you're lucky, Mardi Gras Indians might show up. It's also a great spot for live storytelling and stand-up comedy.

Siberia (MAP: 17 P58 **B3**, *siberianola.com*) is known for its raucous metal shows, but it also has punk, indie and other eclectic bands. Be sure to order from the food pop-up Que Pasta, which makes killer sandwiches and loaded pupusas.

See Folk Art

ART STUDIO

MAP: 18 P58 **E5**

The unofficial city slogan 'Be Nice or Leave' is found on signs all over New Orleans, but it all originates here in the Bywater, at **Dr Bob's Studio** (*@drbobart*). Walk through the gate, past bizarre monsters and snarky statements, before entering the famous folk artist's studio where Dr Bob and his partner Lisa sell psychedelic paintings of legendary musicians framed in old bottle caps, adorned with local symbols like alligator swamp-scapes. Plenty of 'Be Nice or Leave' paintings – Dr Bob first saw the message when buying cigarettes in old African American juke joints – are also for sale.

Walk the Underground Art Scene

WALKING TOUR

You won't find many murals in the French Quarter, but the Marigny and Bywater are filled with gorgeous pieces from top local and international artists, including one you might've heard of: Banksy. Learn the backstory about the art on the walls, under your feet and on the telephone poles on a walking tour with **NOLA Art Walk** (*@nolaartwalk; $30*). Guide Tyler Van Dyke and his team are tapped into New Orleans' graffiti scene,

ARCHITECTURE IN THE MARIGNY

Most houses in the Marigny are painted in toy-house pastels and feature decorative accents outside. Many are Creole cottages that were first built in the 1800s by French immigrants and free people of color. These homes are generally built to the edge of the property line and have four interconnected chambers, each with an opening (a door or window) to the side of the house to allow for a degree of airflow.

FREE PEOPLE OF COLOR

Long before the Civil War, New Orleans had the South's largest population of free Black people. They were known as *les gens de couleur libres*, or 'free people of color' in Creole New Orleans. Enslaved people who learned a trade were often allowed to hire themselves out and earn enough money to buy their freedom. During French and especially Spanish rule, free people of color enjoyed a relatively high level of acceptance and developed thriving communities. By the mid-19th century, however, they faced growing oppression, and many fled north before the Civil War began in 1861.

with artists sometimes teaming up with the tour to offer workshops; 10% of ticket sales go to support new art projects.

Embark on an Art Crawl GALLERIES

The Marigny and Bywater have numerous small art galleries and studios, especially on St Claude Ave. They're generally not open to the public unless you make an appointment, so the best way to visit is on the second Saturday of the month, when the galleries swing open their doors for free expositions from 6 to 9pm.

The list of galleries changes, but some mainstays include **Aquarium** (MAP: 19 P58 **E4**; *@aquariumgallery; by appointment 504-982-0314*), a water-themed artist collective in a historic Bywater house; **Antenna** (MAP: 20 P58 **G4**; *antenna.works*), one of NOLA's oldest and largest art collectives; **Farrington-Smith Gallery** (MAP: 21 P58 **A4**; *farringtonsmith-gallery.com*), a 'low-brow' gallery with art from the owners' wide community of friends; **The Front** (MAP: 22 P58 **H4**; *nolafront.org*), home to eclectic art and a bar in the backyard; and the **Bywater Museum of Unnatural History** (MAP: 23 P58 **C4**; *thebmuh.com*), a room of curiosities and contest-winning dioramas.

Hey, Stella! CINEMATIC BUILDING

MAP: 24 P58 **B5**

In *A Streetcar Named Desire*, Tennessee Williams' Broadway play and Hollywood film, Blanche DuBois rides a New Orleans streetcar named, you guessed it, Desire, to stay with her sister Stella and her husband Stanley. The address of the house where Stanley dramatically screams, 'Hey, Stella!' is 632 Elysian Fields Ave in the Marigny. The building at the address is now a vintage shop, **Little Wing & Co**. But before you go there and shout out Stella's name, know that the building doesn't look much like the house in the film, which was actually shot in California. Save your anguished cries instead for the annual Tennessee Williams Literary Festival in March, which holds a Stella Shouting Contest.

Feel the Power of Community SHOPS, YOGA & VOODOO

MAP: 25 P58 C3

In the wake of Hurricane Katrina, community members came together to dream up ways that recovery funds could be used not just to rebuild after the storm, but to create a sustained community. One of their ideas was the **Healing Center** *(neworleans healingcenter.org)*, which opened in 2011. The art-filled building is a hodgepodge of businesses and services that cater for the community's economic, spiritual, emotional, psychological, physical and cultural needs. That means there's a grocery co-op, low-cost hair salon, yoga studio, gym, **Second Story Gallery** *(secondstorygallery nola.org)*, and voodoo and new age paraphernalia shop, the **Island of Salvation Botanica** *(islandof salvationbotanica.com)*.

Stroll the Greenery PARKS & WATERFRONT

Crescent Park (MAP: 26 P58 E5)is a favorite local spot for running, strolling or simply enjoying some quiet time while taking in the views of the Mississippi. Enter over the enormous Rusty Rainbow (an arched bridge) at Piety and Chartres Sts, or at the steps at Marigny and N Peters Sts, and watch the fog blanket the nearby skyline. A 1.4-mile promenade meanders past fragrant gardens and an angular metal-and-concrete conceptual 'wharf' (placed next to the burned remains of the former commercial wharf).

Another neighborhood favorite is **Markey Park** (MAP: 27 P58 F5), which is a popular spot for Bywater families. There's a playground here, and a big lawn to let younger kids run off some energy.

A few blocks from there, a formerly empty lot has been transformed by its Bywater neighbors into **Clouet Gardens** (MAP: 28 P58 E5), a tiny park filled with murals. Performances, concerts and neighborhood get-togethers are frequently held here, and it's a favorite with local families.

See p58 for map of locations

Best Places for...

$ Budget $$ Midrange $$$ Top End

Eating

Breakfast & Bakeries

Alma $$
29 E4
Hype-worthy brunch and Friday dinner from award-winning Honduran chef Melissa Araujo. *8am-3pm daily, 5-10pm Fri*

Elizabeth's $$
30 F5
Big Southern breakfasts that will cure a hangover, plus Dr Bob's artwork for décor. *8am-2:30pm Thu-Tue*

Ayu Bakehouse $
31 B4
Louisiana pastries including boudin boys and muffuletta breadsticks. *8am-3:30pm Wed-Sun, to 2pm Mon & Tue*

Bywater Bakery $
32 F5
Neighborhood meet-up with fabulous baked goods, such as Chantilly cakes. Live music on weekends. *8am-3pm Tue-Mon*

Cafes

Petite Clouet Cafe $
33 E5
Dogs love this cute neighborhood cafe, and so do humans. Great coffee, snacks and wi-fi. *7am-5pm*

Honey's $
34 C3
Stylish all-day cafe with vintage 1920s' vibes, tasty bagels and specialty coffee. *7am-9pm Tue-Sat, to 3pm Sun & Mon*

St Coffee $
35 D3
Come to photograph the tile art of a saint outside. Stay for coffee, breakfast burritos and donuts. *7am-4pm*

Satsuma $
36 F5
Bohemian, exposed-brick cafe with a shaded garden and sandwiches for breakfast and lunch. *8am-2pm*

Comfort Food, Pizzas & Burgers

Buffa's $$
37 A4
Esplanade Ave restaurant and bar since 1939, serving burgers and Louisiana classics like boudin balls and red beans. *10am-2am*

Frady's $
38 F4
Breakfasts, po'boys and plates in a food grocery that hasn't changed since 1972. Cash only. *7:30am-3pm Mon-Fri, from 10am Sat*

Sneaky Pickle $$
39 F4
Mostly vegan pub with excellent mac 'n' cheese, smoked tempeh Reubens and carrot juice Micheladas. *11am-9:30pm Wed-Mon*

Pizza Delicious $$
40 F5
New York thin-crust pies and pasta from a renovated garage. *11:30am-9pm Tue-Thu & Sun, to 10pm Fri & Sat*

Original Slap Burger $
41 C4
Smash burgers with tasty sauces inside Marie's Bar. *5-10pm Mon-Thu, noon-midnight Fri & Sat, noon-9pm Sun*

Elysian Bar
JOEL BALSAM/SHUTTERSTOCK

International Fare

St Roch Market $$

42 C3

Food court in an 1875 market with cuisine from Cuba, Italy, Malaysia and elsewhere. *7am-9pm Sun-Thu, to 10pm Fri & Sat*

Jamaican Jerk House $$

43 H4

Lines out the door for tasty jerk chicken and oxtail. *11:30am-6pm Tue-Thu, to 9pm Fri & Sat, noon-4pm Sun*

Budsi's $$

44 A4

Chef Budsaba Yantabam shares her family's northern Thai recipes inside a former church. *11am-9pm Sun-Thu, to 10pm Fri & Sat*

Fine Dining

Acamaya $$$

45 E4

The small plates at chef Ana Castro's Mexican seafood restaurant have generated lots of buzz. *5-9:30pm Thu-Mon*

Paladar 511 $$$

46 C5

Thinking Italian? Opt for fresh pasta and pizza in a former shoe factory. *5:30-9:30pm daily, plus 10am-2pm Sat & Sun*

N7 $$$

47 E3

Memorable French, Japanese and fish tapas served in a romantic, twinkly lit garden. *5-9pm Mon-Thu, 11:30am-2:30pm & 5-10pm Fri-Sun*

Saint-Germain $$$
48 E4
Michelin-style 10-course tasting menu enjoyed in a dining room. Stay for after-dinner drinks on the patio. *5-11pm Thu-Mon*

Drinking

Cocktails & Cooking

Elysian Bar
49 C4
The hotel bar at Peter & Paul features exquisitely stylish décor. *7am-11pm Sun-Thu, to midnight Fri & Sat*

Bar Pomona
50 C3
Jam shop turned cocktail-and-small-plates bar, plus weekend brunch. *4-9pm Thu, Fri & Mon, 10-9pm Sat, 10am-2pm Sun*

Neighborhood Classics

Anna's
51 D4
Marigny institution inside a Creole mansion with cocktails, pop-up eats and themed parties. 4pm-2am Mon-Fri, from noon Sat & Sun

Bud Rip's
52 F4
This longstanding red-lit dive attracts a hip crowd. Look out for the food pop-ups. *3pm-3am Sun-Fri, from 1pm Sat*

Parleaux Beer Lab
53 H5
Great craft-beer list, some made with fruit plucked from its biergarten. 3-9pm Mon-Thu, noon-10pm Fri & Sat, 1-8pm Sun

Faubourg Wines
54 D3
Affordable new- and old-world wines enjoyed in the bar ($2 corking fee). Tastings Wednesdays 5-7pm. *noon-7pm Tue-Sun*

Dive Bars

R Bar
55 A5
Inevitable stop near the French Quarter that spills onto the street. *3pm-3am Mon-Thu, to 5am Fri, noon to 5am Sat, to 3am Sun*

Checkpoint Charlie
56 B5
This dive bar has late-night haircuts on Monday nights. Oh, NOLA. *24hrs*

Shopping

NOLA Originals

She Comes in Peace
57 B3
Part salon, part handmade alien-themed costumes – where else would you find something like this but in NOLA? *noon-6pm Tue-Thu, 10am-6pm Fri-Sat*

Bywater Bargain Center
58 E5
A treasure trove of vintage clothing, cheap records, antiques, trunks, tchotchkes and Oaxacan alebrijes. *11am-6pm Thu-Mon*

We Bite
59 D3
Pick up a carnivorous plant and attend a workshop on how to care for them. *10am-5pm Tue-Sun*

Books & Records

Euclid Records
60 F5
Beloved two-floor record shop with jazz classics and more. It's featured in the video for 'Record Shop' by local band Video Age. *11am-6pm*

Baldwin & Co
61 B3
There's a focus on Black writers at this bookshop and cafe. Look out for book launches. *7am-6pm*

See p87
for eating and
drinking listings

Explore CBD & Warehouse District

Amid high-rises and wide, traffic-heavy roads, the Central Business District (CBD) still harbors a few historic buildings, especially near Lafayette Square. This was the heart of the former Faubourg St Mary, one of the first new tracts to be added as New Orleans outgrew the small French Quarter. In the 19th century, it morphed into the American Sector as new arrivals flocked to New Orleans following the Louisiana Purchase. Adjoining the CBD is the Warehouse District. Once linked to port commerce and manufacturing, its stolid brick buildings have since been transformed into galleries and museums as part of the city's growing Arts District.

Getting Around

On Foot

This area is fairly walkable. If you're traveling from the French Quarter to the WWII Museum or the Ogden, it's just under a mile from Canal St.

Bicycle

There are numerous Blue Bikes Nola stations in the CBD. For a system-wide map and bike access, download the app.

Streetcar

The St Charles and Canal streetcars run along their respectively named streets. The Riverfront runs from the Quarter to the Outlet Collection at Riverwalk. The Rampart connects the Union Passenger Terminal to Elysian Fields Ave.

CBD skyline at night
SEAN PAVONE/SHUTTERSTOCK

THE BEST

IMMERSIVE HISTORY National WWII Museum (p76)

ART COLLECTION Ogden Museum of Southern Art (p80)

ANIMAL ENCOUNTERS Audubon Aquarium (p80)

GAME-DAY EXPERIENCE Caesars Superdome (p82)

PANORAMA Vue Orleans (p86)

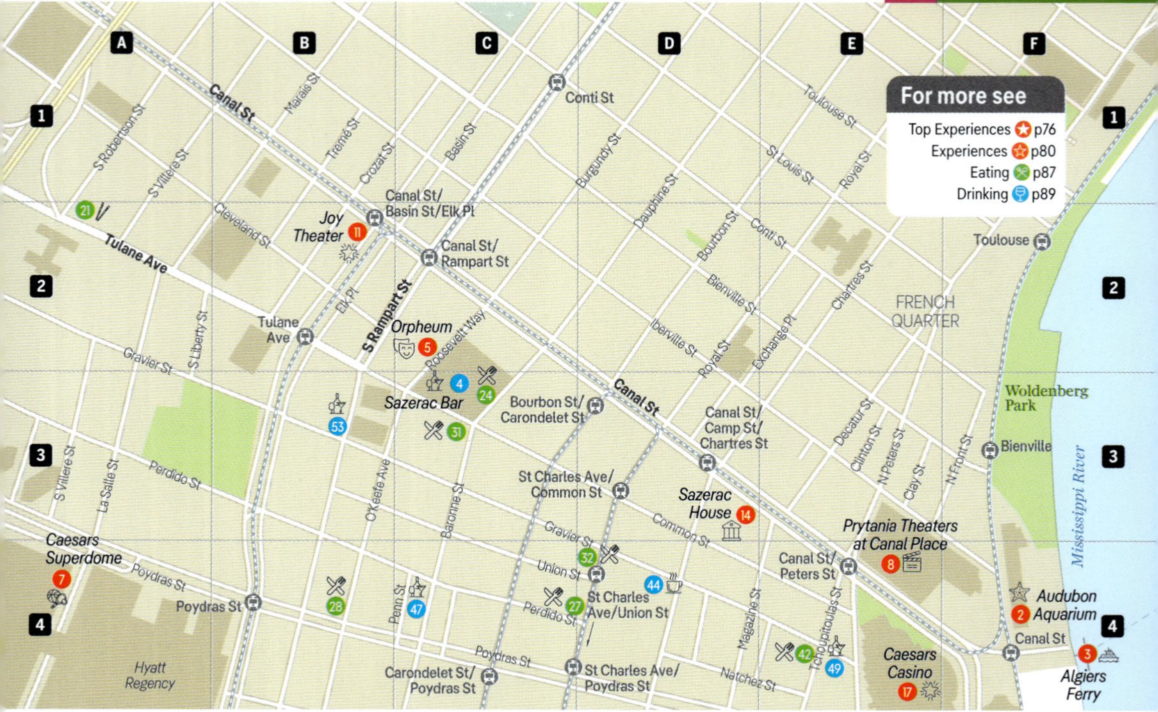
For more see
Top Experiences p76
Experiences p80
Eating p87
Drinking p89
Canal St
Tulane Ave
S Rampart St
FRENCH QUARTER
Woldenberg Park
Mississippi River
Joy Theater 11
Orpheum 5
Sazerac Bar 4
Sazerac House 14
Prytania Theaters at Canal Place 8
Audubon Aquarium 2
Algiers Ferry 3
Caesars Casino 17
Caesars Superdome 7
Hyatt Regency
Canal St/ Basin St/Elk Pl
Canal St/ Rampart St
Tulane Ave
Bourbon St/ Carondelet St
Canal St/ Camp St/ Chartres St
St Charles Ave/ Common St
Canal St/ Peters St
St Charles Ave/Union St
St Charles Ave/ Poydras St
Carondelet St/ Poydras St
Poydras St
Conti St
Toulouse
Bienville
Canal St
S Robertson St
S Villere St
Marais St
Treme St
Crozat St
Basin St
Burgundy St
Dauphine St
Bourbon St
Conti St
St Louis St
Toulouse St
Royal St
Chartres St
Bienville St
Iberville St
Exchange Pl
Decatur St
Clinton St
N Peters St
Clay St
N Front St
Cleveland St
Elk Pl
Roosevelt Way
S Liberty St
Gravier St
Perdido St
La Salle St
O'Keefe Ave
Baronne St
Common St
Union St
Penn St
Magazine St
Tchoupitoulas St
Natchez St

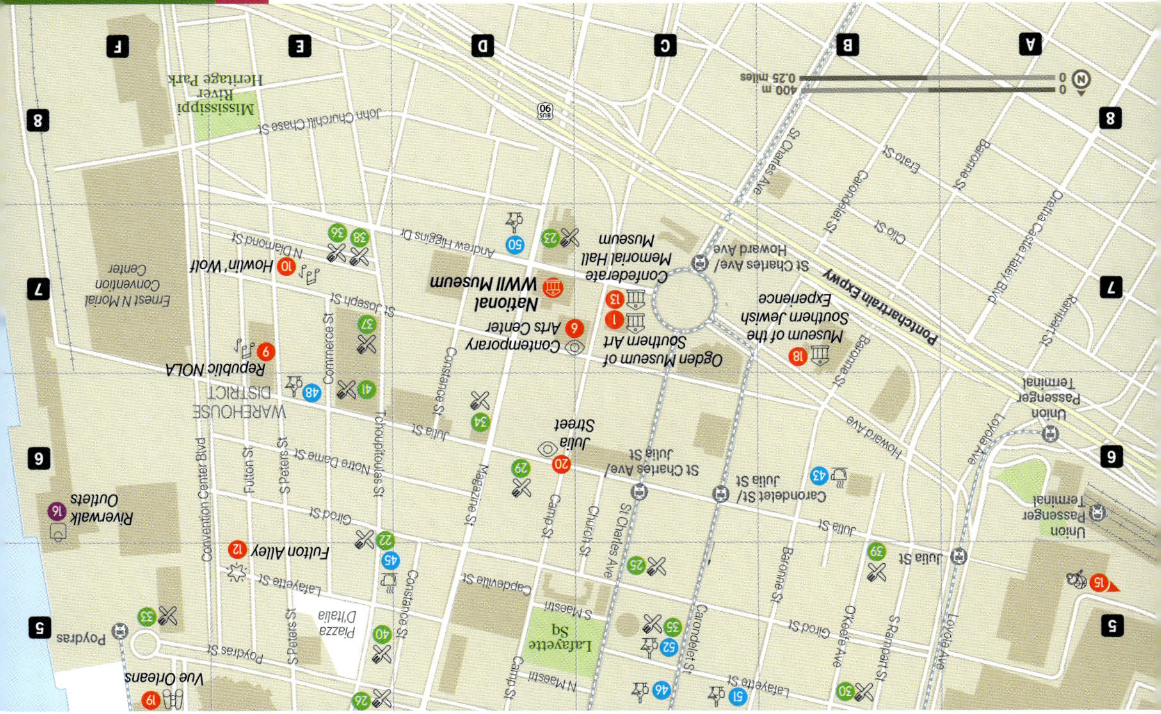

A
B
C
D
E
F
5
6
7
8
400 m
0.25 miles
Vue Orleans
Poydras
Poydras St
Riverwalk Outlets
Convention Center Blvd
Fulton St
S Peters St
Fulton Alley
Lafayette St
Piazza D'Italia
Girod St
Notre Dame St
Tchoupitoulas St
Constance St
WAREHOUSE DISTRICT
Republic NOLA
Commerce St
Ernest N Morial Convention Center
Howlin' Wolf
N Diamond St
St Joseph St
Julia St
Magazine St
Camp St
Church St
Capdeville St
Lafayette Sq
N Maestri
S Maestri
Julia Street
Contemporary Arts Center
National WWII Museum
Andrew Higgins Dr
St Charles Ave
St Charles Ave/ Julia St
Carondelet St
Carondelet St/ Julia St
Ogden Museum of Southern Art
Confederate Memorial Hall Museum
St Charles Ave/ Howard Ave
Museum of the Southern Jewish Experience
Baronne St
Howard Ave
O'Keefe Ave
S Rampart St
Loyola Ave
Union Passenger Terminal
Pontchartrain Expwy
Clio St
Erato St
Oretha Castle Haley Blvd
Rampart St
John Churchill Chase St
Mississippi River Heritage Park

★ TOP EXPERIENCE

National WWII Museum

The National WWII Museum is a grand facility that drops you straight into the action, presenting a thorough analysis of history's largest war. Wall-sized photographs capture the confusion of D-Day; riveting oral histories tell stories of survival; immersive experiences engage; and humanized artifacts and war strategies educate.

MAP P74 **D7**

PLANNING TIP
The museum also runs guided tours that offer deeper insights into WWII. A two-hour highlights tour costs $30 extra, while Into the Vault is a private, curator-led foray into rarely displayed artifacts *($225)*. Book online.

Scan this QR Code for prices, opening hours and special events.

The Road to Berlin

The museum's exhibits are displayed across multiple grand pavilions. The Road to Berlin takes you from the war's first battles in North Africa to the hard-fought combat on the edge of the German capital. The multimedia experience features recreated battle settings that evoke the sights (crumbling villages, wintery forests) and sounds (explosions, firing of artillery) that Allied soldiers faced. You'll get a taste of the rocky desert landscape of Tunisia in attempts to gain a foothold in the Mediterranean, then it's onward to Sicily and the conquest of Palermo. Scenes from the Air War include personal stories from Tuskegee Airmen, along with videos, personal items and oral histories.

The Road to Tokyo

The Road to Tokyo's highlight is the Pacific theater, treading a route that begins in the days after Pearl Harbor and ends with the unconditional Japanese surrender in Tokyo Bay. A replica bridge of the USS *Enterprise* gives a view (via video screens) of planes taking off over enemy waters. Another section puts you in the jungles of Guadalcanal in the Solomon Islands during the first ground assault by US forces. The galleries end with the harrowing bombing campaign of Japan, culminating in the horrifying

RITU MANOJ JETHANI/SHUTTERSTOCK

use of atomic weapons on Hiroshima and Nagasaki. The final room recreates the surrender ceremony of Japanese envoys aboard the USS *Missouri*.

Beyond All Boundaries

The must-see film of the museum is *Beyond All Boundaries*, which presents a 4D insight into America's involvement in the war – on a 120ft-wide screen. Get ready for rumbling seats and a dusting of snowflakes, with Oscar-winning actor Tom Hanks narrating the evocative 48-minute experience. It runs on the hour from 10am to 4pm daily.

Final Mission

Final Mission is an immersive experience that places visitors in the USS *Tang* submarine. Amid smoke, explosive sounds and a jerking floor, you'll get a taste of the intricacies and dangers of underwater warfare during a 1944 patrol mission.

TAKE A BREAK

There are six different restaurants, including **Rosie's on the Roof** (p89). The nostalgic **Jeri Nims Soda Shop** *(8am-3pm)* serves breakfasts, sandwiches and milkshakes.

WALKING TOUR

Walk the CBD's Art & Architecture

Elegant parks, public sculptures and impressive 19th-century buildings dot New Orleans' second-oldest district, formerly known as the American Sector. You'll see vestiges of the past on this memorable meander – from a soaring cathedral and former city hall to imaginative artwork commemorating hurricane victims.

START	END	LENGTH
Gallier Hall	Scrap House	1 mile; 1½ hours

1 Old City Hall

Architect James Gallier Sr designed the Greek Revival **Gallier Hall** on St Charles Ave, dedicated in 1853. It served as New Orleans' city hall until the 1950s and far outclasses the city's current one (a few blocks away). The building is only open for private functions and is a focal point for Mardi Gras parades, many of which promenade past the grandstand.

2 Landscaped Square

Beautifully landscaped **Lafayette Square** feels like a slice of Europe. Originally known as Place Gravier, it was renamed in honor of the Revolutionary War hero Marquis de La Fayette following his visit to New Orleans in 1825. Free Wednesday evening concerts *(5pm-8pm)* are held here from mid-March to mid-May.

3 Ecclesiastical Grandeur

You can see more of James Gallier Sr's fine work at the soaring **St Patrick's Church** up the street. He took on the project after two other architects failed to master the complex problems of building in swampy terrain. Modeled on Exeter Cathedral, the somewhat sober Gothic façade hides an exuberant interior. The striking murals behind the altar were completed in 1841 by the young artist Leon Pomarede.

4 Former Beacon for the Blind

One of the most unusual buildings in the CBD is the **Camp Street Lighthouse**. Built in the 1920s when novelty architecture was all the rage, the structure was modeled after a lighthouse on Lake Pontchartrain and served as a workshop for the blind, which provided employment – making brooms – to visually impaired residents.

5 Artsy District

Turn left onto Julia Street to arrive in the epicenter of the Arts District, with over a dozen galleries housed in the old brick buildings. One of the most prominent is **Arthur Roger Gallery**, which represents several dozen artists from the South. Keep an eye out for pieces by Demond Melancon, a Mardi Gras Indian chief who makes elaborate beaded patches and suits. You might also see dreamy, environmentally concerned works by Jacqueline Bishop or wetland scenes featuring natural materials by Cajun artist Jonathan Mayers.

6 Remembering Katrina

Cut through the small **Mississippi River Heritage Park** to reach a tiny plaza set with one of the city's most evocative public sculptures. Entitled Scrap House, it depicts a small battered cottage perched in the crook of an oak tree and pays homage to the victims of Hurricane Katrina. Artist Sally Heller created the work using recycled materials.

EXPERIENCES

Visit the Ogden Museum of Southern Art

ART MUSEUM

MAP: 1 P74 C7

One of the city's most engaging museums, the **Ogden** *(ogden museum.org; adult/child $11/6)* houses impressive artwork that illuminates unique facets of the South in all its complexity. Rotating exhibitions showcase thought-provoking fare, from New Orleans street photography to overlooked Appalachian communities.

Set in a five-story building, it's best to start on the top floor and work your way down, with the views from the 5th floor contextualizing this artistic cache.

The 3rd floor is dedicated to the permanent collection. Early portraits date back to the 18th century, with exquisite works by French artists Jean Joseph Vaudechamp and Jacques Amans, followed by Paul E Poincy, a Native New Orleanian who became the most celebrated painter of the late 1800s. The 19th century was also a high point for landscape painting in the South, with beautiful sunsets over the bayous and captivating 'rural' landscapes; see Lulu King Saxon's emblematic *Uptown Street* (1890).

Check online for upcoming events and Ogden After Hours.

Meet the Penguins

AQUARIUM

MAP: 2 P74 F4

At the **Audubon Aquarium** *(audubonnatureinstitute.org; adult/child $40/35)*, you can see some 3600 animals (over 250 different species) in exhibits dedicated to the Mississippi River, the Gulf of Mexico, the Caribbean Sea and the far-off Amazon rainforest.

The impressive Great Maya Reef lures visitors into a 30ft-long tunnel running through a 'submerged' Mayan city, now home to unique fish. There's also a penguin colony, a seahorse gallery, a touch tank and eerily lit displays of otherworldly jellyfish. In the Mississippi River Gallery, look for the white alligator, along with frogs, turtles and other bayou critters. Even more surprising is the Amazon section, with fauna of air, land and water – including toucans, tree sloths and piranhas. The aquarium's showpiece is the 400,000 gallon Gulf of Mexico tank – home to sharks, sting rays, sea turtles and some massive fish.

The aquarium is fairly compact, and you can see it all in about 90 minutes or less. As a member of the Association of Zoos and Aquariums (AZA), Audubon adheres to rigorous standards when it comes to animal welfare and conservation.

Hop on a Boat to Algiers

FERRY RIDE

MAP: 3 P74 F4

If you want a river experience without the fuss (and price tag) of an organized tour, hop aboard the **Algiers Ferry** *(pedestrians &*

cyclists one-way $2). Boats depart from the foot of Canal St every 30 minutes. The ride takes about 10 minutes and gives you a fine view of the Quarter as you sail across the muddy Mississippi. Once you reach the other side, you can take a spin along the Mississippi River Trail, which runs atop the levee, or take a stroll through the streets of the historic neighborhood of Algiers Point, perhaps stopping to refuel at the much-loved **Barracuda Taco Stand**.

Drink in a 1930s' Classic

COCKTAIL BAR

MAP: 4 P74 **C3**

Walking through Roosevelt Hotel's chandeliered lobby and into the polished glow of the **Sazerac Bar** *(therooseveltneworleans.com)*, you feel as though you've stepped back into a well-heeled era of hushed wheeling and dealing by politicos and high rollers. With its art deco murals, subdued lighting and plush couches, the Sazerac evokes all the moody atmosphere of the 1930s. Ask the bartender to point out the bullet hole in the wall – according to urban legend, it was made by an assassination attempt on then Louisiana governor Huey Long (who was later killed by a gunman in the state capital in Baton Rouge). In truth, the mark was made by the accidental discharge of a six-shooter when a group of drunken Texas oil men were carousing at the bar in 1938.

Catch a Concert at the Orpheum

PERFORMING ARTS VENUE

MAP: 5 P74 **C2**

Opened in 1921, the **Orpheum** *(orpheumnola.net; tickets from $35)* is a beaux arts beauty that has undergone many incarnations – vaudeville stage, movie house – and now the home of the Louisiana Philharmonic Orchestra. It also hosts ballets, jazz and R&B concerts, with numerous local and international artists drawn to the the restored glory of the venue. Keep an eye out for movie screenings with live orchestras and the odd Taylor Rave – a midnight concert featuring danceable Taylor Swift remixes and mashups.

See Artistic Pioneers

EXHIBITIONS & PERFORMANCES

MAP: 6 P74 **D7**

From the outside, the **Contemporary Arts Center**, aka the CAC *(cacno.org; adult/child $10/free)*, is fairly unassuming. But once inside, you'll enter an impressive setting complete with soaring ceilings and metal and wood accents, which make a fine backdrop to the center's multidisciplinary programing. Exhibitions lean into provocative topics and themes related to social justice, and you can also catch film screenings, dance shows, concerts, performances by resident artists and engaging discussions. In all, it's an essential first stop when exploring the Warehouse District's arts scene.

BEST DOWNTOWN ENTERTAINMENT

Prytania Theaters at Canal Place

MAP: 8 P74 **E4**

Owned by a local family, this nine-screen cinema shows blockbusters, classics and indie features.

Republic NOLA

MAP: 9 P74 **E7**

A renovated 19th-century warehouse transformed into an atmospheric space and home to an eclectic lineup of live concerts.

Howlin' Wolf

MAP: 10 P74 **E7**

One of the city's better-known venues for rock, New Orleans-style jazz, comedy and the odd burlesque show.

Joy Theater

MAP: 11 P74 **B2**

The 1200-seat art deco-style theater hosts acts ranging from hip-hop to rock and EDM mini festivals.

Fillmore New Orleans

see 17 P74 **E4**

One of the newer concert venues downtown, the Fillmore is a beautifully designed space for catching alt-rock, R&B and country bands.

Watch a Saints Game

FOOTBALL STADIUM

MAP: 7 P74 **A4**

Fresh off a five-year $450-million renovation, the **Caesars Superdome** *(caesarssuperdome.com)* is looking more dapper than ever. By night, you can't miss its ethereal glow, which looms like an oversized galactic mothership in the heart of the city. The 72,000-seat arena was named Caesar's Superdome in 2021, when Caesars Entertainment bought the stadium's naming rights to tie in with their newly acquired casino, also in the CBD. Despite this, it's still the fabled ground where the much-loved Saints play their home football games. For some fans, the year officially begins not at midnight but on New Year's Day when two top college teams play in the Sugar Bowl. The dome also stages big concerts (Taylor Swift, the Rolling Stones) and has hosted seven NFL Super Bowls – the most recent in 2025.

Make it a Games Day

BOWLING ALLEY

MAP: 12 P74 **E5**

Fulton Alley *(fultonalley.com; $50 per hour)* is the downtown spot for bowling (while sipping cocktails and munching Creole-influenced pub grub in a vaguely Prohibition-era atmosphere). Apart from working the lanes, you can also shoot pool, play table football or throw some darts. All ages are welcome during the day, but it's ages 21 and up after 8pm. Come during happy hour *(4pm-6pm, Wed-Fri)* for half-off bowling. Reserve ahead.

See Confederates in the Attic

MUSEUM

MAP: 13 P74 **C7**

Tattered gray uniforms, rebel swords and faded diaries – the **Confederate Memorial Hall Museum** *(confederatemuseum.com; $15)* features the memorabilia of those who fought for the Confederacy. Opened in 1891, this place remains a mere 'collection of things' rather than a contemporary, interpretation-driven educational museum; the lack of material relating to slavery is jarring.

Discover NOLA's Drink History

INTERACTIVE MUSEUM

MAP: 14 P74 **D3**

Located on Canal St, **Sazerac House** *(sazerachouse.com; admission free)* is a three-story museum and distillery that pays tribute to the Sazerac (New Orleans' most famous cocktail) while also taking visitors on a drink-minded tour into the past. The building, which dates from the mid-1800s, makes a memorable setting for the experience.

Start off on the 3rd floor, where interactive exhibits trace the early days of tippling in New Orleans at the turn of the 20th century and touch on some of the intriguing ingredients that made the Sazerac (and other drinks) such a success. Work your way down to the 2nd floor, which focuses on rum drinks, before visiting the 1st-floor distillery, where you'll see how rye is made.

You'll be able to sample products along the way (if you're 21 and older, of course). For something more in depth, book a guided tour *($20 including cocktail samples)* or attend one of the specialty tasting sessions *(from $30)*.

Cheer for the Pelicans

PRO BASKETBALL

MAP: 15 P74 **A5**

Right next to the Superdome, the **Smoothie King Center** *(smoothie kingcenter.com)* plays host to the Pelicans, New Orleans' pro basketball team. Apart from watching the Pels tear it up on the court – led by superstar power-forward Zion Williamson – you can catch some great concerts in the 17,000-seat arena. Childish Gambino, Jelly Roll and Master P have all performed here in recent years, along with comedians like Katt Williams and Jeff Dunham.

Run with the Bulls

JULY THRILLS IN THE CBD

Reason enough to visit in July, **San Fermin in Nueva Orleans** *(nolabulls.com)* is a riotously fun event modeled on the Running of the Bulls in Pamplona. As in Spain, participants don their festive whites with red sash and red neckerchief, lace up their running shoes and then run through the streets pursued by bulls. Only here, the 'bulls' are horn-wearing roller-derby girls wielding plastic bats, which are used to whack the bottoms of any runners they come across. The action happens early in the morning, followed by lots of drinking and celebration. Reserve tickets for the after-party online.

Shop the Riverwalk — OUTLET STORES

MAP: 16 P74 **F6**

The **Riverwalk Outlets** *(riverwalkneworleans.com)* is the place to browse name brands at discounted prices. Over 50 different shops fill this retail center along the riverfront, with well-known stores like Coach, Ralph Lauren and Skechers. Fashion hunters shouldn't overlook Nordstrom Rack, while those looking for something with more local flavor should head to women's clothing shop Nola & Co and Mardi Gras Masquerade. The Riverwalk also has over a dozen eating and drinking spots. It's mostly fast food, beignets (fried pastries dusted with powdered sugar) and ice cream, though for something more memorable, you're only a short hop from Drago's (p87).

Play Roulette — CASINO

MAP: 17 P74 **E4**

All manner of fun is welcome in the Big Easy, and that extends to **Caesars Casino** *(caesars.com/caesars-new-orleans)*, a 115,000-sq-ft behemoth. Formerly known as Harrah's, the property was rebranded and given a $435 million makeover in 2024, complete with a soaring 340-room hotel tower and some great new restaurants. Welcome to New Orleans, Nobu!

There are lots of ways to chase after good fortune here, from working the slot machines to ponying up to the blackjack table. If you're not interested in all that gambling business, focus your attention on the new food hall, which features dishes from some of New Orleans' top chefs, as well

THE STEAM-POWERED ECONOMIC BOOM

For early European settlers, the Mississippi River proved too unruly to serve as a viable route inland – until the advent of the steamboat in the early 1800s. Up until then, flatboats delivered goods downriver, but since they couldn't go upstream, they were typically dismantled after reaching their terminus in New Orleans. After the first steamboat journey from Pittsburgh to New Orleans in 1811, the shipbuilding boom was on, quickly followed by burgeoning economic growth. Trade rose from under $3 million to $54 million between 1800 and 1840, and the city's population soared from under 10,000 in 1800 to over 150,000 by 1860.

Caesars Casino
WILLIAM A. MORGAN/SHUTTERSTOCK

as classic cocktails. You can also catch a show in the **Fillmore** (p82; *thefillmorenola.com*).

Discover Southern Jewish Heritage

MUSEUM

MAP: 18 P74 B7

At the **Museum of the Southern Jewish Experience** *(msje.org; adult/child $15/10)*, you can learn what it means to be Jewish in the American South. Start off by watching the 10-minute film, which explores the unique dichotomy of combining Jewish and Southern traditions – typified by a meal of bagel and lox with a side of grits. Next, you can explore the history of early Jewish colonists in the South (dating as far back as 1585) and the many roles they played, in fields from politics to sales. True to name, the museum doesn't focus exclusively on New Orleans or even Louisiana, so you'll get an interesting overview of immigration to the region – particularly through Galveston, TX, which for a time was something of the Ellis Island of the South.

Don't miss the Ruth Bader Ginsburg float that's used by the

Krewe de Mishigas, one of the two parading Jewish groups of Mardi Gras.

Admire New Orleans' Best Views

OBSERVATION DECK

MAP: 19 P74 **F5**

The city's finest panorama lies on the upper level observation decks of **Vue Orleans** *(vueorleans.com; adult/child $30/24)*. It's set atop the newish Four Seasons Hotel, and the experience begins on the ground floor with interactive exhibits. A huge map stretches out on massive screens, and you need only point to an area to get a snapshot of NOLA's history, culture and geography. Afterwards, you'll continue to a theater for a short film that illuminates more of the New Orleans story.

The high-tech tour continues on your ascent, where lively videos play in the elevator as you ride up to the 33rd floor. Once there, the view opens before you, while yet more interactive screens allow for explorations of the city's rich culture. One flight up, you can enjoy open-air views over the Mississippi and the city stretching along its curving banks. A bar serves cocktails, ice chicory coffees and other refreshments from the 34th-floor cafe.

Go Gallery Hopping on Julia Street

ART DISTRICT

MAP: 20 P74 **D6**

Sometimes referred to as Gallery Row, **Julia Street** is the heart of the Warehouse Arts District *(arts districtneworleans.com)*, with a smattering of galleries dotting the old buildings along the one-way thoroughfare. Once an industrial area in the late 19th century, it fell on hard times in the mid-20th century, but saw rebirth following the 1984 World's Fair.

The best stretch of the block lies between St Charles and Tchoupitoulas, and things are liveliest on the first Saturday of the month, when most of the district's 17 galleries host special exhibitions *(6pm-9pm)* and pour glasses of wine for thirsty art-gazers.

Galleries are free to visit and generally open from Tuesday to Saturday from about 10am to 4/5pm.

See p74 for map of locations

Best Places for...

$ Budget $$ Midrange $$$ Top End

Eating

Lunchtime Favorites

Pho Tau Bay $
21 A2
Join the lunchtime crowds for delicious *banh mi* (Vietnamese sandwiches) and pho. *11am-7pm Mon-Fri*

St James Cheese Company $
22 E6
Heavenly cheesy sandwiches with caramelized onions. *11am-6pm Mon-Sat, 11am-4pm Sun*

American Sector $$
23 D7
This ode to the Greatest Generation looks like a 1940s' diner and features juicy burgers and Southern fare. *11am-2pm*

Domenica $$
24 C3
Stylish but unpretentious, Domenica has first-rate wood-fired pizzas, tempting antipasti and imaginative pasta dishes. *11am-10pm*

Creole Cooking

Herbsaint $$$
25 C5
Another hit from celebrated chef Donald Link, the small menu here is near perfection. *11:30am-9:30pm Mon-Fri, 5pm-10pm Sat*

Mother's $
26 E5
Opened in 1938, this classic diner has all the favorites: po'boys, jambalaya and crawfish *étouffée*. *7am-10pm*

Luke $$$
27 C4
Elegantly minimal bistro whips up elevated Creole cooking, from ragout of roasted rabbit to speckled trout amandine. *7am-10pm*

Copper Vine $$$
28 B4
Equal parts gastropub and wine bar, come here for a good mix of decadent mains and shared plates. *11am-9pm*

Fusion & Asian Fare

Carmo $$
29 D6
Expect deep tropical influences, from Asia to South America. Try Peruvian sashimi or Burmese tea-leaf salad. *5-10pm Mon, 11am-10pm Tue-Sat*

Maypop $$$
30 B5
Creative fusion of the South and Southeast Asia via dishes like coconut-crusted Gulf drum with curried tomato and okra compote. *5pm-9pm*

Namaste Nola $$
31 C3
Despite the hotel setting, it fires up beautiful Indian fare, including a rich paneer tikka masala. *11am-3pm & 5pm-10pm Thu-Tue*

Lufu Nola $$
32 D4
Stylish choice for artful Indian classics like chili chicken with an Indo-Chinese sauce. *11:30am-2:30pm & 5pm-9:30pm Thu-Tue*

Seafood

Drago's $$
33 F5
Come for charbroiled oysters that drip with butter, garlic and parmesan after kissing an open fire. *11:30am-10pm*

Mother's (p87)
WILLIAM A. MORGAN/SHUTTERSTOCK

Pêche $$$

34 D6

One of New Orleans' best seafood restaurants lets the high-quality ingredients speak for themselves. *11am-10pm*

Seaworthy $$$

35 C5

Brilliantly executed seafood, from yellowfin tartare to seared scallops, plus a legendary raw oyster selection. *4pm-11pm*

Carnivore's Delight

Cochon Butcher $$

36 E7

Convivial lunch crowds gather over sandwiches and whimsical cocktails in this charcuterie shop. *11am-10pm*

La Boca $$$

37 E7

The place for unique Argentine steaks cooked to perfection. Order the four-course tasting menu. *5:30pm-10pm Mon-Sat*

Cochon $$

38 E7

Donald Link pays homage to his Cajun culinary roots, serving meats smoked and wood-fired to perfection. *11am-10pm*

Marrow Steak $$$

39 B5

The hot opening of 2024, Marrow Steak has mouth-watering steaks, including a famous tomahawk for two. *4pm-10pm*

Fine Dining

Compère Lapin $$$
40 E5
Nina Compton heads this outstanding mashup of Caribbean–Italian and Creole cooking. *5:30pm-9pm*

Nobu $$$
see 17 E4
New in 2024, the famous Japanese–Peruvian restaurant delivers unforgettable hits, like toro tartare with caviar. *5pm-10pm*

Emeril's $$$
41 E6
Be dazzled by the 10-course tasting menu here, featuring artful dishes like lobster gumbo. *5:30pm-9:30pm Tue-Sat*

Restaurant August $$$
42 E4
Reserve a table at this romantic 19th-century tobacco warehouse that's known for its French Creole cuisine. *5pm-9pm*

Drinking

Coffee Culture

Mammoth Espresso
43 B6
Dazzling tile floors, indoor and outdoor seating and great coffee made from house-roasted beans. *7am-3pm*

Fourth Wall
44 D4
The neighborhood's most atmospheric coffee shop has a soothing plant-filled courtyard. *7am-3pm Mon-Sat, 8am-3pm Sun*

Nova Espresso
45 E5
The Alabama transplant makes a strong, satisfying cold brew, which you can enjoy in the sleek, minimal interior. *7am-3pm*

Cocktails

Bar Métier
46 C5
Red walls, shelves full of books and globe chandelirs create an enchanting setting for bespoke cocktails. *4pm-midnight*

Baronness on Baronne
47 C4
The woman-owned lounge adds a dash of verve to the CBD, with house-made syrups. *4:30pm-11pm Wed-Sun*

Jolie
48 E6
One of the Warehouse District's most stylish drinking dens, old-world Jolie has plush booths and playful artwork. *4pm-11pm Wed-Mon*

Polo Club Lounge
49 E4
Dark wood and leather chairs give a clubby vibe to this buttoned-up spot – sip cognac during the nightly live jazz. *11:30am-11pm*

Rooftop Bars

Rosie's on the Roof
50 D7
Atop the Higgins Hotel, this vintage industrial spot has outdoor seating and creative bar snacks. *4pm-10pm*

The Pool Club
51 C5
Come at golden hour (*4-6pm weekdays*) for drink specials atop the tropical-themed Virgin Hotels New Orleans. *10am-10pm*

Rooftop at the Barnett
52 C5
The 9th-floor rooftop of the former Ace Hotel has a garden-like vibe, with memorable views. *11am-10pm*

Ingénue
53 B3
Above the Troubadour Hotel, this place features some of the best views over the CBD from its 17th-story perch. *5pm-11pm Thu-Sun*

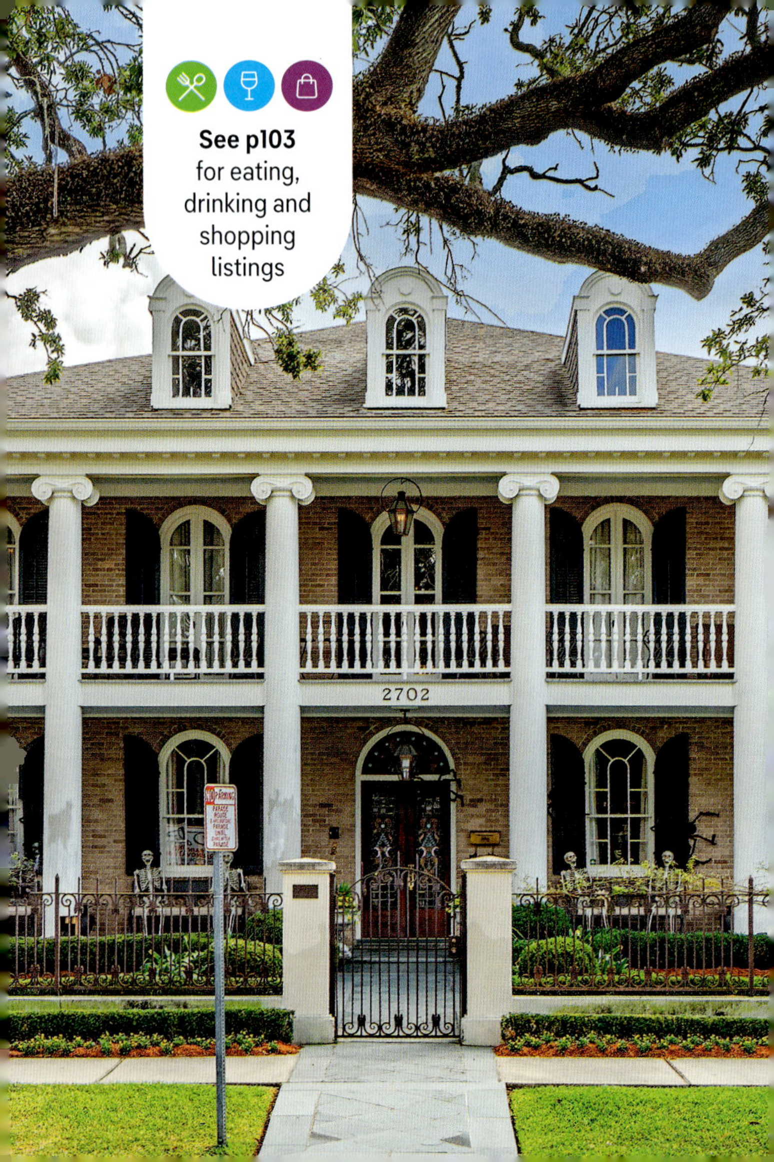

See p103 for eating, drinking and shopping listings

Explore
Garden District, Lower Garden & Central City

Among the most photogenic corners of the city, the Garden District exudes Old Southern excess with its historic mansions, lush greenery, chichi bistros and upscale boutiques. Between the Central Business District (CBD) and the Garden District, the Lower Garden District is somewhat like its upriver neighbor but not quite as posh. There's a slightly more bohemian vibe here, and plenty of bars and restaurants for all budgets. Nearby Central City is very much in transition. While there are large stretches of urban blight, there is also a dynamic concentration of community activist organizations rebuilding what was once one of the city's most important African American neighborhoods.

Getting Around

On Foot

The Lower Garden and Garden Districts are among the city's loveliest neighborhoods for strolling. Trees provide shade, and when you need a break, just stop at the cafes on Magazine Street.

Streetcar

The St Charles Ave Streetcar runs from Canal St to the Lower Garden and Garden Districts. Key stops are Jackson, Washington and Louisiana.

Bus

For Magazine Street, take Bus 11 from Canal St or the CBD. It stops every few blocks on Magazine and continues to Uptown.

Architecture in the Garden District
TRAVELVIEW/SHUTTERSTOCK

★ **THE BEST**

FINE DINING Commander's Palace (p96)

COOKING COURSE Southern Food & Beverage Museum (p97)

QUIRKY COLLECTION Great American Alligator Museum (p99)

ROOFTOP BAR Hot Tin (p99)

CRAFT BREWERY Urban South (p100)

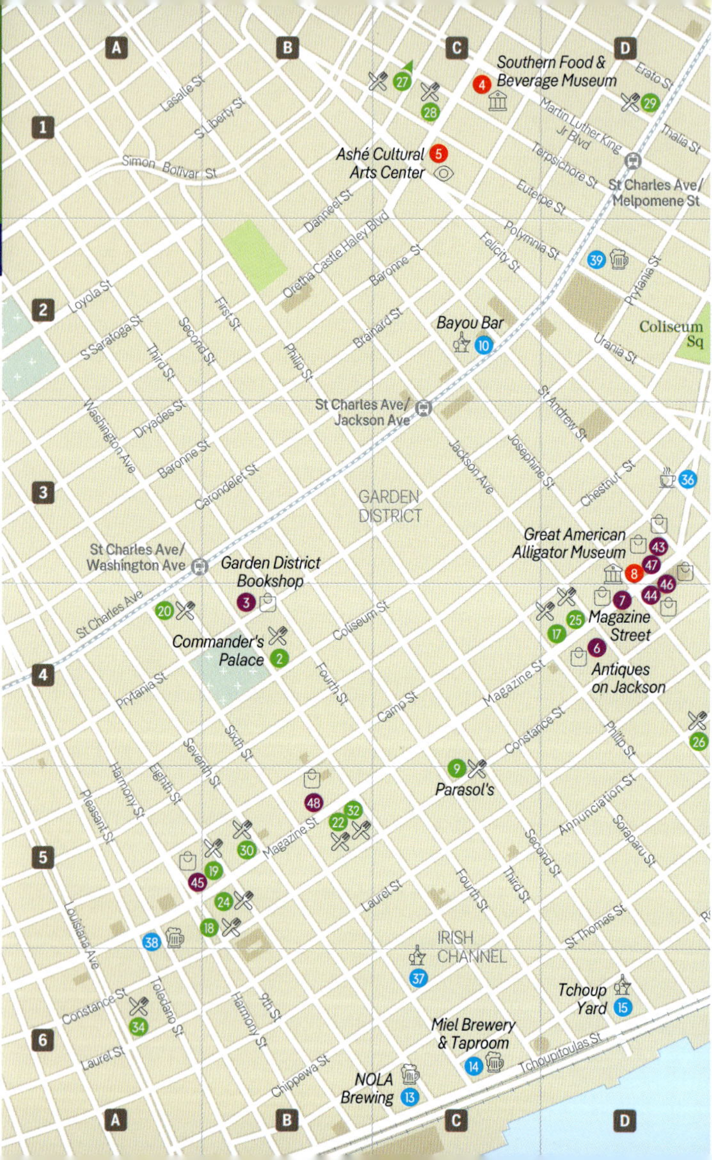
A
B
C
D
1
2
3
4
5
6
Southern Food & Beverage Museum
4
27
28
29
Ashé Cultural Arts Center
5
Erato St
Thalia St
Martin Luther King Jr Blvd
Terpsichore St
Euterpe St
St Charles Ave/ Melpomene St
Polymnia St
Felicity St
39
Prytania St
Coliseum Sq
Urania St
Lasalle St
S Liberty St
Simon Bolivar St
Danneel St
Oretha Castle Haley Blvd
Baronne St
Brainard St
Bayou Bar
10
Loyola St
S Saratoga St
Third St
Second St
First St
Philip St
St Charles Ave/ Jackson Ave
St Andrew St
Josephine St
Jackson Ave
Washington Ave
Dryades St
Baronne St
Carondelet St
GARDEN DISTRICT
Chestnut St
36
Great American Alligator Museum
43
47
8
46
44
7
St Charles Ave/ Washington Ave
Garden District Bookshop
3
St Charles Ave
20
Commander's Palace
2
Coliseum St
Magazine Street
25
17
6
Antiques on Jackson
Prytania St
Fourth St
Camp St
Magazine St
Constance St
Philip St
26
Sixth St
Seventh St
Eighth St
Harmony St
Pleasant St
9
Parasol's
48
32
22
Annunciation St
Soraparu St
Magazine St
30
19
45
24
18
38
Louisiana Ave
Laurel St
Fourth St
Third St
Second St
IRISH CHANNEL
St Thomas St
37
Tchoup Yard
15
Constance St
Toledano St
Harmony St
9th St
34
Laurel St
Miel Brewery & Taproom
14
Tchoupitoulas St
Chippewa St
NOLA Brewing
13

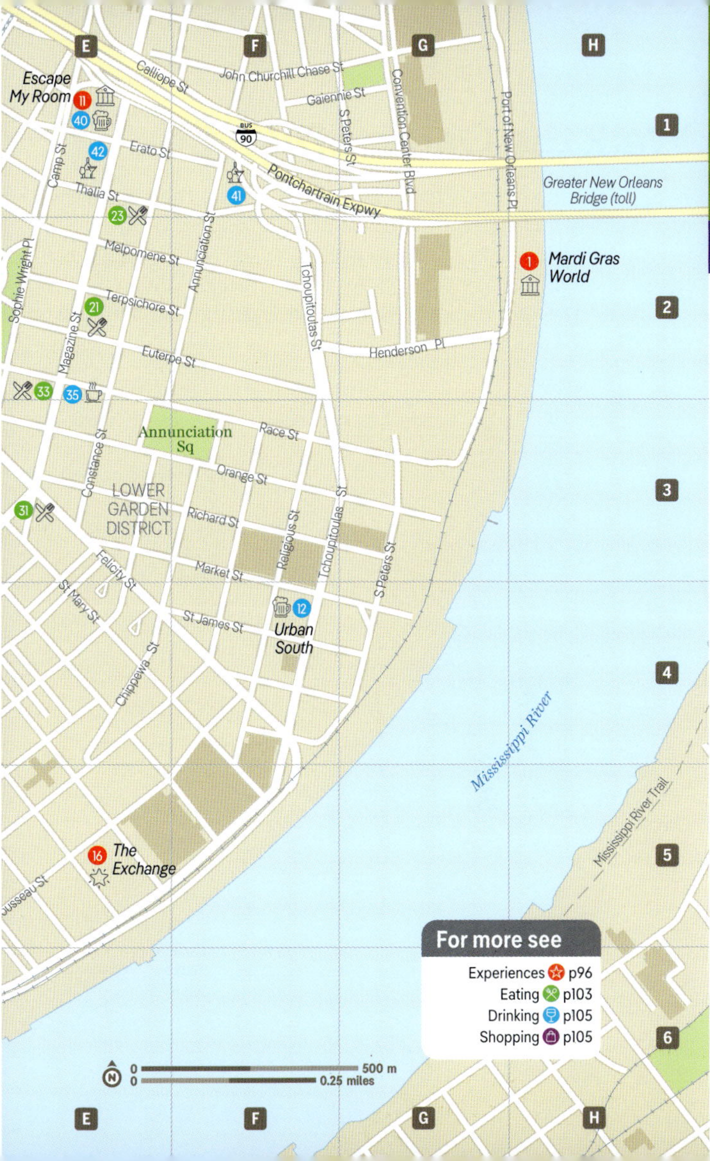
Escape My Room
Mardi Gras World
The Exchange
Urban South
Annunciation Sq
LOWER GARDEN DISTRICT
Greater New Orleans Bridge (toll)
Pontchartrain Expwy
Mississippi River
Mississippi River Trail
Calliope St
John Churchill Chase St
Gaiennie St
Erato St
Thalia St
Melpomene St
Terpsichore St
Euterpe St
Race St
Orange St
Richard St
Market St
St James St
Felicity St
St Mary St
Camp St
Magazine St
Sophie Wright Pl
Constance St
Annunciation St
Tchoupitoulas St
S Peters St
Convention Center Blvd
Port of New Orleans Pl
Henderson Pl
Religious St
Chippewa St
Rousseau St
For more see
Experiences p96
Eating p103
Drinking p105
Shopping p105
500 m
0.25 miles

WALKING TOUR

Walk the Garden District

Explore the beauty and fright (!) lurking within the streets of the Garden District, New Orleans' most atmospheric neighborhood. The best way to get to the start of this walk is by hopping aboard the St Charles Avenue streetcar. You'll feel the hands of time spin backwards as you roll past grand houses and centuries-old oak trees.

START	END	LENGTH
The Rink	Goodrich-Stanley House	1 mile; 1½ hours

1 Literary Iconic

After disembarking at Washington St, you can enjoy the (unearthly?) quiet as you leave St Charles behind and head towards the river. Walk one block south to **The Rink**, an 1880s' skating rink turned 21st-century mini-mall. Inside is one of New Orleans' best indie bookstores. At the **Garden District Book Shop**, you'll find fiction and history by local authors, as well as coffee-table books on Mardi Gras and other facets of New Orleans culture. This was where the late novelist Anne Rice used to host the launches for her various vampire blockbusters.

2 Macabre Moodiness

Cross the street and walk down Washington Ave. On your right, **Lafayette Cemetery No 1** exudes a strong sense of subtropical Southern Gothic. The stark contrast of moldering crypts and gentle decay with the forceful fertility of the fecund greenery is incredibly jarring. It's a place filled with stories – of German and Irish immigrants, deaths by yellow fever, social societies doing right by their dead – that pulls the living into New Orleans' long, troubled past.

3 Cinematic Mansion

As you stroll past the cemetery, note the flamboyant turquoise and white colors announcing the **Commander's Palace**, one of New Orleans' best old-school Creole restaurants. Turn left onto Coliseum St. At the end of the block, you'll reach the **McKnight Marinoni Nolan House**, which played a starring role in *The Curious Case of Benjamin Button*.

4 Vampires in the House

Continue along Coliseum and turn right on First St. If the home at **1239 First St** looks like it could house an aristocratic vampire, you're on the right track. This home, known as the Brevard-Rice House, was the late author Anne Rice's residence from 1989 to 2004.

5 American Horror Story

Make your way to Jackson Ave and turn left. At 1410 Jackson Ave, you'll find the massive **Buckner Mansion**, which served as a stand-in for Miss Robichaux's Academy for Exceptional Young Ladies in season 3 of *American Horror Story*.

6 African Explorations

Turn left back on Coliseum and walk another six-ish blocks. Facing Coliseum Park, at 1729 Coliseum St is the historic **Goodrich-Stanley House**, dating from the 1830s. It was once owned by the British-born merchant Henry Home Stanley, whose adopted son, Henry Morton Stanley, won fame for finding the missing Scottish explorer Dr David Livingstone, one of the first Westerners to see Victoria Falls.

EXPERIENCES

Get a Taste of Mardi Gras

BUILDING TOUR

MAP: 1 P92 **H2**

We dare say **Mardi Gras World** *(mardigrasworld.com; adult/child $22/14)* is one of the happiest places in New Orleans by day, but at night it probably turns into a terrifying fun-house. It's all those faces: dragons, clowns, kings and fairies, leering and dead-eyed. That said, we love touring Mardi Gras World – the studio-warehouse of Blaine Kern (Mr Mardi Gras) and family, who have been making jaw-dropping parade floats since 1947. Tours last about 90 minutes.

There are never fewer than 2000 props in the inventory, and the company builds about 50 or 60 new ones each year. Kern learned the trade from his father and passed it down to his sons.

If you're staying at a hotel in the CBD or near Canal Street, you can get here by taking the company's free shuttle. These pick up at 10 different stops in the area. There's no schedule: just call to arrange a pick-up (*504-361-7821*).

Feast at Commander's

FINE DINING

MAP: 2 P92 **B4**

Commander's Palace *(commanderspalace.com)* is a dapper spot that wows with white-linen dining rooms, decadent dishes and attentive Southern hospitality. The nouveau Creole menu shifts, running from crispy oysters with brie-and-cauliflower fondue to pecan-crusted Gulf fish. The dress code adds to the charm: no shorts or T-shirts, and jackets preferred at dinner. It's a very nice place, and lots of fun.

Owner Ella Brennan takes pride in her ability to promote her chefs to stardom, with Paul Prudhomme and Emeril Lagasse among her alumni. And note that some of that stiff-upper-lip formality is put on; the lunch special, after all, is the 25¢ martini. Reservations required.

Curl Up with a New Book

BOOKSTORE

MAP: 3 P92 **B4**

Maybe it's pouring rain outside, or you just need a break from the heat; whatever the weather, **Garden District Bookshop** *(gardendistrictbookshop.com)* makes a pleasant spot to while away the afternoon in the company of some great stories. Knowledgeable staff can help you find some new reading material, and there are lots of selections on local and regional books – fiction, history, cookbooks, children's books and more. GDBS hosts regular author readings and book signings, and the neighboring cafe is a charming spot to get working on that novel of yours.

Celebrate Southern Cooking

CULINARY MUSEUM

MAP: 4 P92 C1

You don't have to be a gourmet or mixologist to enjoy the **Southern Food & Beverage Museum** *(southernfood.org; adult/child $12/ free)*, aka SoFAB. This made-from-scratch destination celebrates Southern cooking and cocktails with exhibits sourced from every state south of the Mason–Dixon line.

There's lots to look at as you wind your way around the large hall. You'll learn about the larger-than-life figure of Al Copeland, a high-school dropout who ended up creating Popeye's Chicken. There's a big section on coffee (and chicory – a beloved New Orleanian addition), red beans and rice, and the city's big culinary personalities. Don't miss the whimsical Katrina Deli, with its Heckuva Job Brownies and Levee Leak Soup. Other exhibits highlight the food heritage of other states, including a recreated barbecue shack from Mississippi and seafood delicacies from Florida. There's also a section on cocktails. Allow about 45 minutes to an hour to explore the museum.

Cook Creole & Cajun

COOKING CLASS

see 4 P92 C1

Apart from its fine cooking and cocktail displays – and having the best acronym of any museum we've ever visited – **SoFAB** also hosts cooking classes in a fun, informal environment. A 2½-hour hands-on Creole cooking class costs about $115, and you'll learn how to prepare a hearty jambalaya, smothered okra and tomato, and bananas Foster. Another similarly priced option focuses on Cajun cooking, where you'll master a proper Cajun gumbo. Needless to say, one of the best parts of the experience is enjoying your handiwork at the end. Classes are currently offered three times a week, starting at around 11am. Reserve online.

LEGENDARY GUMBO

Candi Vanardo, sous chef at the **Deelightful Roux School of Cooking** (*chefdeelavigne.com*), gives insight into New Orleans' quintessential dish: 'The secret to gumbo is your roux and filé. If there is no filé – ground sassafras leaves – then it is not gumbo. The filé gives it a certain taste, texture and color. They say gumbo should look like the Mississippi River, and filé has that ability to make it kind of dredgy. What you put in it depends on where you grew up. For me, there's going to be seafood, smoked sausage and hot sausage.'

Experience the Culture of the African Diaspora
GALLERY & CULTURAL CENTER

MAP: 5 P92 **C1**

An important anchor for the community, the **Ashé Cultural Arts Center** *(ashenola.org)* has a regular lineup of performances, art exhibitions, movie screenings and lectures with an African, African American or Caribbean focus. There's always something going on, especially in October when Ashé hosts its big rooftop festival with food, music, cocktails and vibrant cultural programing. Check the online calendar for other happenings.

See the Signs of Simon
ART & ANTIQUE SHOP

MAP: 6 P92 **D4**

Local artist Simon Hardeveld has made a name for himself by painting groovy signs that hang like artwork in restaurants across New Orleans. Spend enough time in the city and you'll soon begin to recognize the distinctive stars, dots and sparkles that fill the spaces between letters on colorfully painted signs such as 'Laissez Le Bon Temps Rouler' ('Let the Good Times Roll'). Find his work at **Antiques on Jackson**, a shop that Hardeveld owns with his wife Maria. True to name, the store has lots of items from yesteryear, including furniture, lamps, ceramics and other homeware.

Stroll the Indie Boutiques of Magazine Street
SHOPPING

MAP: 7 P92 **D4**

Magazine Street is by far New Orleans' best shopping strip. As a center for commercial activity, it begins in the Lower Garden District, near the intersection with Felicity St. From here, you can follow Magazine west all the way to **Audubon Park** and shop or window browse in antiques stores and boutiques almost the entire way. On the second Saturday in May,

ORETHA CASTLE HALEY

Central City's main thoroughfare is named for Oretha Castle Haley (1939–87), founding member of the Congress of Racial Equality, which led the fight in the Civil Rights Movement of the 1960s. Castle Haley organized boycotts of segregated businesses and was one of the main leaders of local civil-disobedience and direct-action campaigns. She promoted voter registration in New Orleans and in rural Louisiana and helped desegregate many places, including Charity Hospital and citywide playgrounds. Later, she managed the campaign of Dorothy Mae Taylor, who, in 1971, became the first Black woman to be elected as a state legislator in Louisiana.

the district hosts a champagne stroll, where bubbly flows, stores stay open late – till 9pm – and live music fills the air.

Discover a Newfound Love for Alligators GALLERY & KITSCH STORE

MAP: 8 P92 D3

Small in size, the **Great American Alligator Museum** (*gatormuseum.com; entry by donation*) is a delightful place to learn more about Louisiana's favorite reptile. You'll see some massive taxidermy on display, along with folk art (check out the flamingo alligator), vintage clips from kitschy films about alligator people and plenty of curiosities – like the alligator hide used as armor by ancient peoples. There's even a juvenile alligator in the aquarium.

Raise a Glass with New Friends IRISH BAR

MAP: 9 P92 C5

Parasol's is the anchor of the Irish Channel, serving as community center, nexus of gossip and watering hole. It's first and foremost a bar, but you can order some of the best po'boys in town from the barebones seating area in the backroom – the roast beef is a messy, juice-filled conduit of deliciousness, while the firecracker shrimp has a delicious burn. There are also picnic tables along the sidewalk – great for those less steamy days.

Note that the bar is open until around 1am (2am on weekends). The later you come, the crazier the characters – this spot has the vibe of an old-school New Orleans neighborhood dive. Parasol's is also St Patrick's Day headquarters, when a huge block party occurs on the street on March 17.

Catch Jazz at Bayou Bar MUSIC BAR

MAP: 10 P92 C2

Tucked inside the Pontchartrain Hotel, **Bayou Bar** (*thepontchartrainhotel.com*) is a historic slice of New Orleans. Music has always been an integral part of Bayou Bar, and since it first opened in 1946, it's been a draw for music stars, including Frank Sinatra and Jimmy Buffett. The bar also has a deep connection to the city's most beloved institution: it was here in the late 1960s that the Saints football franchise was christened.

Bayou is one of the best places in the neighborhood to catch evening jazz performances. Shows kick off at 8pm and 9.45pm from Tuesday to Saturday, and all ages are welcome (those under 18 must be seated at a table and not the bar). There's no cover charge.

Enjoy Sunset Cocktails ROOFTOP BAR

see 10 P92 C2

On the uppermost floor of the Pontchartrain Hotel, **Hot Tin** (*thepontchartrainhotel.com*) is one of New Orleans' best rooftop bars outside of the CBD. The indoor space channels a 1940s vintage glam, complete with old sepia photographs on the walls, dramatic curtains and a pressed tin ceiling. Most first-time visitors, however, are immediately drawn to the view. Tables out on the balcony provide a fine 270-degree panorama over downtown and the twin spans arcing across the Mississippi River. Unlike Bayou Bar in the same building, Hot Tin is strictly 21s and up. It's also first come, first served, so go early to score a prime spot with a view (the bar is open from 2pm to midnight). The drinks are pricey but well made, and you can sip creative concoctions like the Rita Hayworth (tequila, chipotle chilis, apricots and lime).

Solve a NOLA Riddle ESCAPE ROOM

MAP: 11 P92 **E1**

Even if you've done an escape room before, it's worth challenging yourself to solve these puzzles before the time runs out in one of the city's best-loved interactive adventures. **Escape My Room** *(escapemyroom.com; from $116)* is set in an atmospheric house on Camp St, and it has four different rooms, each set with antique furnishings and vintage curios. Scenarios involve solving a murder, finding a hidden treasure and discovering the secrets of an inventor's attic. You and up to seven other guests have between 45 minutes and an hour to use your sleuthing skills to puzzle your way out. All ages are welcome (kids must be accompanied by adults), and the provided costumes can help you get in the mood. Prices are based on the number of participants, and you can save a bit from Mondays through Thursdays. Reserve in advance.

Sip a Quality Microbrew FAMILY-FRIENDLY BREWERY

MAP: 12 P92 **F4**

In an industrial dystopia of warehouses and concrete jungle, you'll find a big convivial beer hall packed with happy folks and, yes, laughing kids. Family-friendly **Urban South** (*urbansouth.com*) keeps a rotating array of beers on tap. Try hits like the Holy Roller (a hazy juicy IPA), the Lime Cucumber Gose (a sour wheat beer) and the light, easy-drinking Paradise Park, or see what's on hand in their seasonal lineup. More cutting-edge options are the THC-infused Driftees, the effects of which Urban South describes as imparting 'a relaxed and floaty feeling, like you're drifting away on a cloud.' The food truck Urban Smash, meanwhile, serves burgers, fries and other snacks.

Urban South hosts lots of events, including football-game screenings, trivia nights, bingo and the odd juxtaposition of yoga plus beer or books and beer. For more insight into the brewery, come on Friday or Saturday (hourly from noon to 3pm) for a brewery tour.

Miel Brewery & Taproom
ZIMMYTWS/SHUTTERSTOCK

These cost $12 and include a 16oz pour and a souvenir glass.

Discover a Craft-Beer Pioneer MICROBREWERY

MAP: 13 P92 C6

One of the trailblazers of the city's craft beer renaissance, **NOLA Brewing** *(nolabrewing.com)* set up shop on an industrial stretch of Tchoupitoulas back in 2009, and it's been a hit ever since. The taproom is the go-to spot for trying the 20 or so different beers on draft – from a refreshing Blonde to more daring seasonal selections (try Just Like Grandma's Strawberry Rhubarb Sour). If you want to sample a few, get a flight. The pizzas here get almost as much love as the beers, with delicious pies that go well with the craft brews. There's also free live music most Friday and Saturday nights (7pm-10pm).

Sip the Tropics MICROBREWERY

MAP: 14 P92 C6

Miel Brewery & Taproom *(mielbrewery.com)* is a favorite of NOLA's beer connoisseurs for its excellent small-batch brews that aren't afraid to push boundaries. Flavors from the Tropics appear front and center in beers like the Flor de Jamaica, a sour ale brewed with hibiscus, sea salt and cinnamon. Another intriguing favorite is Golden Boi, a juicy pale ale with unique hops (amarillo and sabro) that give it a citrus-like kick.

But for truly experimental sipping, leave all that behind for rotating rarities like La Ventana (a Central American lager made with honey malt and flaked corn) or Paleta de Mango (a fruited sour with mango and tamarind). As with most other brew spots in New Orleans, kids and dogs are welcome, and the patio is a great place to be after the sun goes down. Check their online calendar to see which pop-up food vendors will be there when you pass through. Lobster rolls, Indian-Creole, Filipino and Brazilian fare feature here regularly.

Join the Backyard Party

MICROBREWERY

MAP: 15 P92 **D6**

Another enticing drinking spot on Tchoupitoulas, the **Tchoup Yard** *(tchoupyard.com)* is best known for its sprawling backyard setting. You can sip on a frozen cocktail, craft beer or nicely chilled rosé while enjoying the evening at picnic tables under the trees. There's also creative Tex-Mex fare when hunger strikes. Entrance (and parking) is on 2nd St.

Play Pickleball

SPORTS & RECREATION

MAP: 16 P92 **E5**

Pickleball has taken the US by storm, and New Orleans has likewise fallen under the spell. If you'd like to keep up your game while you're in town, head to **The Exchange** *(theexchangenola.com)*. New in 2023, this is the city's first dedicated pickleball center, offering six indoor courts (in blessed air-conditioning) and one outdoor court, along with a full bar to help improve (maybe?) your swing. Courts cost $48 an hour, or come on weekdays before 5pm when the cost drops to $40. Reserve ahead.

See p92 for map of locations

Best Places for...

$ Budget $$ Midrange $$$ Top End

Eating

Bakeries, Donuts & Pastries

District $
17 D4
One of several locations in New Orleans, District serves up outstanding doughnuts, with toppings like fresh raspberries. *7am-9pm*

Levee Baking Company $
18 B5
Fabulous baked goods, from buttery almond croissants to flatbread with caramelized onions. *8am-1pm Thu-Sun*

The Vintage $
19 B5
An elegant spot for iced coffee and beignets (fried pastries dusted with powdered sugar), which get the gourmet treatment with flavors like brie with pear. *8am-9pm*

Gracious Bakery $
20 A4
Order a pastry and coffee and grab a seat out front where you can watch the streetcar rattle past. *7am-3pm*

Breakfast & Brunch

Surrey's Cafe & Juice Bar $
21 E2
Colorful neighborhood charmer does outstanding breakfasts, like shrimp and grits. *8am-3pm Thu-Mon*

Ruby Slipper $$
22 B5
One of five in town, spacious, family-owned Ruby Slipper has all the classics to make it a brunch favorite. *7am-2pm*

Birdy's Behind the Bower $$
23 E1
Floor-to-ceiling windows and a garden add to the allure of this upscale spot. *9am-3pm Fri-Sun, 10am-3pm Mon-Thu*

Red Dog Diner $$
24 B5
A farmhouse interior sets the stage for chowing on blueberry pancakes and slow-cooked brisket and hash. *8am-6pm Thu-Mon*

Delis & Sandwiches

Stein's $
25 D4
This famed deli is an unrivaled spot for bacon, egg and cheese bagels, and pastrami on rye. *8am-5pm Tue-Fri, 9am-5pm Sat & Sun*

Turkey and the Wolf $
26 D4
A popular spot with outdoor tables, it does playful reinventions, including an astonishingly good bologna sandwich. *11am-4pm Wed-Mon*

Central City Favorites

Central City BBQ $$
27 C1
The love child of two local chefs with a passion for barbecue and wood smoke. *11am-7pm Mon-Thu, to 9pm Fri-Sun*

Cafe Reconcile $
28 C1
Delicious cooking that creates job opportunities for youth from marginalized communities. *11am-2:30pm Tue-Fri*

Joey K's
ELLIOTT COWAND JR/SHUTTERSTOCK

Creole & Cajun Cooking

Mr Ed's $$

29 D1

Start with the seafood gumbo or charbroiled oysters before proceeding with crawfish *étouffée* and blackened catfish. *11am-9pm*

Joey K's $

30 B5

Going strong since the 1970s, Joey K's is a mainstay for first-rate Creole cooking, with mouthwatering jambalaya. *11am-9pm Tue-Sat*

Gris-Gris $$$

31 E3

Moodily lit Gris-Gris serves elevated Southern cooking in imaginative dishes like sugarcane seared duck. *11am-9pm Wed-Mon*

Fine Dining

Coquette $$$

32 B5

A classy spot with a vintage aesthetic, great wines and Louisiana-sourced cooking. *5:30pm-9pm Mon-Sat*

San Lorenzo $$$

33 E2

St Vincent Hotel's northern Italian restaurant has tasty prawn risotto and handmade pastas. *8am-10pm*

Atchafalaya $$$

34 A6

The brilliant haute-Creole cooking in a laid-back cottage makes Atchafalaya a standout. *9:30am-9pm Thu-Mon*

Drinking

Cafes & Coffeehouses

Mojo Coffeehouse

35 E2

Linger over a well-poured latte and a pastry, with a strong communal vibe. *6am-9pm*

Hivolt

36 D3

Excellent espresso makes Hivolt a must for connoisseurs. Delicious breakfast sandwiches. *7am-5pm Mon-Sat*

Neighborhood Bars

Pete's Out in the Cold

37 C6

Come for the fun crowd, happy-hour deals and pop-up food vendors (grilled cheese, souvlaki). *hours vary*

The Bulldog

38 A5

Dozens of craft beers on tap, hearty pub fare and a tree-shaded patio for taking in the passing street-scene. *11am-1am*

Bars of the Lower Garden District

The Avenue Pub

39 D2

Choose from 40 beers on tap, then grab a table on the balcony or in the backyard and let the night unfold. *11am-1am*

Courtyard Brewery

40 E1

This small-batch brewery produces innovative quaffs; also pop-up food in the courtyard. *4pm-11pm Mon-Thu, 11am-midnight Fri-Sun*

Tell Me Bar

41 F1

This well-hidden natural-wine bar has a beautiful indoor and outdoor design and unusual wines from around the globe. *4pm-11pm*

Barrel Proof

42 E1

A festive, bourbon-centric spot with corrugated iron walls, a long dark-wood bar and fine cocktails with a creative edge. *4pm-1am*

Shopping

Vintage Style

Century Girl Vintage

43 D3

A well-curated selection of new, one-of-a-kind, high-end dresses. *11am-5:30pm Mon-Sat, noon-5:30pm Sun*

Trashy Diva

44 D4

Think vintage pin-up with a modern flourish: boldly patterned dresses and caftans, and Kabuki-inspired loungewear. *noon-6pm Mon-Sat, 1pm-5pm Sun*

Funky Monkey

45 A5

A good selection of fashions from decades past, along with wigs and other costume ideas. *11am-6pm*

Accessories & Souvenirs

Miette

46 D3

Packed with one-of-a-kind jewelry, home goods and artwork, Miette is a bit of whimsical wonderland. *10am-6pm*

Cocoally

47 D3

Possum lovers unite at this cute, cruelty-free shop with lots of T-shirts, gift cards, books and other items emblazoned with the misunderstood marsupial. *10am-6pm*

Zèle NOLA

48 B5

An emporium of locally made jewelry, crafts, homeware, apparel, skincare products and artwork. *11am-5pm Mon-Sat, noon-5pm Sun*

See p121 for eating, drinking and shopping listings

Explore
Uptown & Riverbend

Uptown radiates genteel privilege from its maze of live-oak alleyways that are sundered by Greek Revival mansions, student apartments, candy-colored residential blocks and two universities. And yet, this is still New Orleans, where social strata mix and eccentricities are celebrated. Nurses, teachers and hedge-fund managers all stand in the same coffee line, a way-too-early Mardi Gras party is thrown in August, and even the most aristocratic estates display a yard full of skeletons come Halloween. Two oak-lined avenues, St Charles and Carrollton, are framed by stately mansions and plied by streetcars that seem to trundle straight out of a nostalgic dream.

Getting Around

Bus

Bus 11 runs along Magazine St, from Canal St to Audubon Park. Pick it up at the corner of Canal and Magazine, in front of the Sheraton Hotel.

Streetcar

The St Charles Avenue streetcar travels through the CBD and Garden District and into Uptown/Riverbend.

Car

Metered parking *($2 per hour)* is required along much of Magazine St between 8am and 7pm, Monday through Saturday. Look for free parking on side streets.

Bicycle

A bike lane runs along St Charles Avenue.

THE BEST

DIY TOUR St Charles Avenue Streetcar (p110)

GREEN SPACE Audubon Park (p112)

ANIMAL ENCOUNTERS Audubon Zoo (p113)

CREATIVE COCKTAILS Cure (p117)

LIVE MUSIC Tipitina's (p118)

Magazine Street
WILLIAM A. MORGAN/SHUTTERSTOCK

A
B
C
D
1
2
3
4
5
6
Oak St Brewery
33
Jacques-Imo's Café
5
18
3
19
Carrollton Station
Maple Leaf
4
1
Blue Cypress Books
Levee Path
27
Z'otz
2
St Carrollton Ave/Oak St
Rue de la Course
Cambronne St
Dublin St
S Carrollton Ave
Fereet St
Oak St
Zimple St
Willow St
Plum St
Jeannette St
Birch St
Green St
Hickory St
Cohn St
Spruce St
Panola St
Broadway St
Audubon St
Audubon Blvd
41
Lowerline St
Pine St
Burthe St
Maple St
Hampson St
Burdette St
Adams St
Hillary St
Cherokee St
S Carrollton Ave/St Charles Ave
Newcomb Art Museum
11
6
Hot Stuff
Tulane University Special Collections
12
St Charles Ave
Pearl St
Dominican St
Benjamin St
Hurst St
Newcomb Blvd
Calhoun St
10
Tulane University
13
Loyola University
St Charles Ave/Broadway St
St Charles Ave/Tulane University
Leake Ave
Lowerline St
Pine St
Broadway St
Loyola St
Prytania St
Audubon St
Walnut St
St Charles Ave/Calhoun St
Mississippi River
Benjamin St
23
Skeleton House
Hurst St
Audubon Park Golf Course
Garfield St
Pitt St
Audubon Park
Exposition Blvd
Calhoun St
Henry Clay Ave
Webster St
Prytania St
Perrier St
Coliseum St
Chestnut St
Camp St
Magazine St
Constance St
Patton St
Laurel St
Riverview Dr
Audubon Zoo
East Dr
35
47
37
40
State St
Eleonore St
Nashville Ave
Arabella St
32
Annunciation St
Tchoupitoulas St
9
Frankie & Johnny's
0
1 km
0
0.5 miles
N

For more see
Top Experiences p110
Experiences p114
Eating p121
Drinking p122
Shopping p123
E
F
G
H
1
2
3
4
5
6
90
S Claiborne Ave
State St Dr
Vincennes Pl
Napoleon Ave
Jena St
Cadiz St
Johnson St
Prieur St
Roman St
S Derbigny St
Robert St
Lyons St
Palmer Ave
S Claiborne Ave
Willow St
Clara St
Washington Ave
Magnolia St
Toledano St
Louisiana Ave
Gen Pershing St
State St
Clara St
Nashville Ave
Magnolia St
S Robertson St
Freret St
La Salle St
S Liberty St
Joseph St
Octavia St
Jefferson Ave
Bearcat Cafe
16
Cure
17
High Hat Cafe
15
14
Freret Street Market
Marengo St
Gen Taylor St
Loyola St
S Saratoga St
Danneel St
Dryades St
Baronne St
Carondelet St
Peniston St
Amelia St
Foucher St
Delachaise St
S Saratoga St
Valence St
Cadiz St
Jena St
Napoleon Ave
St Charles Ave/ Nashville Ave
St Charles Avenue Streetcar
Pascal's Manale
8
34
30
St Charles Ave/ Jefferson Ave
Uppertine St
St Charles Ave/ Napoleon Ave
45
44
25
Delachaise
Milton H Latter Memorial Library
24
St Charles Ave
Pitt St
Pitt St
Prytania St
Antonine St
Amelia St
Peniston St
St James Cheese Co
26
29
Perrier St
Coliseum St
Chestnut St
Camp St
UPTOWN
Joseph St
Octavia St
Jefferson Ave
Gen Pershing St
Milan St
Marengo St
Constantinople St
Napoleon Ave
46
Le Bon Temps Roule
20
43
51
22
28
50
Magazine St
48
49
Magazine St
39
42
38
7
Casamento's
Constance St
Dufossat St
Soniat St
Robert St
Uppertine St
Lyons St
Bordeaux St
Valence St
Cadiz St
Jena St
Laurel St
Laurel St
Annunciation St
Leontine St
Valmont St
Bellecastle St
36
21
Tipitina's
31
Tchoupitoulas St

★ TOP EXPERIENCE

St Charles Avenue Streetcar

Some of the grandest homes in the US line St Charles Avenue, shaded by enormous oak trees that glitter with the tossed beads of hundreds of Mardi Gras floats. In the shade, joggers pace themselves while Tulane students flirt with their Loyola friends. Clanging through this bucolic corridor comes the iconic St Charles Avenue Streetcar.

MAP P108 **E4**

PLANNING TIP
A one-way fare on the streetcar is $1.25 (and just 50¢ for kids under 18). You can also pay for tickets and find schedules on Le Pass, the city's transport app.

Scan this QR code to download Le Pass.

Louisiana Avenue to Napoleon Avenue

Running since 1835, the St Charles Avenue Streetcar is the oldest continuously operating streetcar line in the world. The line runs from the CBD to Uptown, with service every 10 to 20 minutes. For the most scenic stretch, hop on at Louisiana Ave and enjoy the view of live oak trees and over-the-top mansions as you make your way westward to Carrollton Ave (a 5-mile journey that takes about 20 minutes or so).

Napoleon Avenue to Jefferson Avenue

It's hard to miss the bright lights of Superior Seafood, which marks where Napoleon Ave crosses St Charles. Heading further 'up' (west) into Uptown, the streetcar passes dozens of mansions. One of these grand homes has since been converted into the **Milton H Latter Memorial Library** (p118), one of the prettiest public buildings in the city. The live oak trees that shade St Charles seem to grow particularly thick here, and many of their lower branches retain beads thrown by krewes (parade marching-clubs) during Mardi Gras.

AEVANSTOCK/SHUTTERSTOCK

Jefferson Avenue to the Riverbend

The streetcar now trundles past Temple Sinai – one of the South's largest synagogues – before cutting through Audubon Park, which is flanked by the campuses of Tulane and Loyola. Where St Charles Avenue ends, the streetcar turns on the riverbend (where the Riverbend neighborhood gets its name) to reach Carrollton Ave.

Carrollton Avenue

Carrollton is like a smaller, more modest version of St Charles: expect more lovely historic homes and plenty of live oak trees. Maple St or Oak St (four blocks farther up Carrollton) are perfect spots to disembark and do some neighborhood exploring.

QUICK BREAK
The streetcar rolls right past the **Camellia Grill** *(camellia grillnola.com)* on 626 S Carrollton Ave. This diner, with its neon-pink façade, has been slinging hash to the hungry since 1946.

★ TOP EXPERIENCE

Audubon Park

Framed by some of the city's grandest residences, Audubon Park is a grand, green space filled with live oak trees, walking and cycling paths, and picturesque waterways. Students lounge on the grass under Spanish moss and friends share outdoor sundowners while joggers lope by.

MAP P108 **C5**

PLANNING TIP
If you've got kids, check out the two playgrounds at the top of the park, adjacent to St Charles Avenue. The one closer to St Charles is for younger children.

The Tree of Life

The southern reaches of the park (across Magazine St) are anchored by one of its loveliest landmarks: the Tree of Life, or the Etienne de Bore Oak. The tree, resembling the hand of Groot bursting through the soil, boasts a 35ft girth and a leafy crown more than 160ft wide.

Oak Strolls

Oak Allée runs from below Magazine St into the northern half of the park. It's a beautiful, veritable hallway of live oaks and a favorite spot for dog walkers and those taking lovers' strolls. Kids will love the rope swings intermittently peppered along the paths.

Water Feature

Olmsted 'Lake' (more of a murky pond) frames much of the southern and eastern section of the park. It features the tiny, inaccessible bird island, where you can see plenty of wading birds chirping and quacking away. Built in 1921, the pretty Newman bandstand overlooks the lake; stand in the center and shout to hear your voice echo thanks to the clever acoustics. As the trail loops around the west end of the park and heads south, it runs adjacent to Walnut St and some of the city's most gorgeous (and expensive) homes.

Scan this QR code for more insights & info.

★ TOP EXPERIENCE

Audubon Zoo

Appropriately enough, Audubon Zoo is located inside Audubon Park. It's a large spot, with sections dedicated to African, Asian and South American landscapes and fauna. Kids will love spotting the elephants and giraffes, and during the summer months, part of the zoo becomes a dedicated water park.

MAP P108 **B5**

Louisiana Swamp

If you're not heading west into Cajun country or going on a swamp tour, this is about the next best thing: a wet wonderland of bald cypresses and Spanish moss carefully landscaped to reflect the natural wonders of southern Louisiana's bayou country. You can see bobcats, alligators, bears and otters here, and you might even spot a red fox chilling on a log in the scrub.

African Savanna

Other highlights of the zoo include a lion enclosure constructed to resemble an East African field-research station, a green area where African wild dogs chase each others' tails, and Monkey Hill, a grassy slope that generations of New Orleans kids have log rolled and somersaulted down with wild abandon. There are also jaguars here, as well as a faux-Mayan temple playground, a dark enclosure for bats and other nocturnal creatures, and walkways – decorated with Mesoamerican lintels and sculptures – that wind past parrots, monkeys and snakes.

Wings of the World

Kids and parents alike love this indoor aviary, where some 60 different feathered species from across the world perch, flutter and warble. Keep an eye out for beauties like the toucan and the hyacinth macaw.

PLANNING TIP
Food options in the zoo are overpriced, but restaurant-dotted Magazine St is a 10-minute walk away. We recommend the **Audubon Clubhouse** *(audubonclubhouse.com)*.

Scan this QR code for prices and opening hours.

EXPERIENCES

Browse for Books

BOOKSTORE

MAP: 1 P108 **B1**

Back in the day, the neighborhood of Carrollton was its own separate village, and the rails were laid for the iconic St Charles Avenue Streetcar largely to connect it to greater New Orleans. Oak St was the main thoroughfare in this 'village,' and while Carrollton is now wholly subsumed into New Orleans, it remains a popular corridor for eating, shopping and exploring Uptown. A good place to start your Carrollton exploring is at **Blue Cypress Books** *(bluecypressbooks.com)*, a wonderful, women-owned independent bookstore that often showcases local literary talent.

Explore Oak Street's Drink Scene

BAR & CAFES

At the corner of Oak and Carrollton sits **Rue de la Course** (MAP: 2 P108 **B1**; *ruedelacourse.com*), one of the most beautiful cafes in the city. The setting alone – a cavernous former bank building – is reason enough to step inside for a look-see. A favorite study spot for Tulane and Loyola students, the cafe whips up strong coffees and filling bagel sandwiches.

While wandering Oak St, pop in for a brew and some board games at **Oak St Brewery** (MAP: 3 P108 **B1**; *oakstbrewery.com*), where parents love to take the kids while they relax with a cold one. With a rotating line-up of creative brews, you'll have to make some tough choices – or sample a few with a flight. And just across from the brewery is **Z'otz** (MAP: 4 P108 **B1**; *zotzcafe.com*), a cafe with an edgy, art-loving vibe, excellent lattes and a shelf full of board games – not a bad spot to seek refuge on a rainy afternoon.

Taste Innovative Cooking

FUSION RESTAURANT

MAP: 5 P108 **B1**

A great spot for a meal (reservations recommended) is the slightly pricey but utterly unpretentious **Jacques-Imo's Café** *(jacques-imos.com)*, a sort of science lab for delicious Louisiana experimentation: think cornbread muffins swimming in butter, steak smothered in blue-cheese sauce, and alligator-sausage cheesecake. It's the sort of place where you could die happy, with butter and heavy sauces sweating out of your pores.

Indulge in Southern Cooking

RESTAURANT

MAP: 6 P108 **C2**

Hot Stuff *(hotstuffneworleans.com)* specializes in that most Southern of gastronomic traditions: the plate lunch, otherwise known as 'the meat and three.' The 'three' refers to the number of veggie or carb sides, making for a meal that should keep you stuffed for the better part of the week. It's a fine place to drop in; no reservations required.

Feast on NOLA's Best Oyster Po'Boy

SANDWICHES

MAP: 7 P108 **G6**

There is never a bad time to eat shellfish in New Orleans. All year long, locals lovingly devour the bounties of the bayou and the goodness of the Gulf, from crabs (summer) and oysters (winter) to crawfish (spring). While shellfish is best during certain seasons, you can often eat it any time of year.

Uptown has some of the best restaurants in the city for a deep dive into the shellfish scene. Making your way from east to west, start at **Casamento's** *(casamentosrestaurant.com)*, where the one word on everyone's lips is 'ersters' (that's New Orleans for 'oyster'). Walk through the 1949 soda-shop interior, cross the tiled floors to a marble-top counter, trade a joke with the shell-shucker and get some freshly shucked oysters, although the oyster loaf (a sandwich of breaded and fried oysters) is also incredible.

Eat a Perfectly Shucked Oyster

RESTAURANT & OYSTER BAR

MAP: 8 P108 **G4**

On Napoleon Ave, you'll find **Pascal's Manale** *(pascalsmanale.com)*, another time warp of a restaurant that feels more like a wood-paneled 1950s' social club. Behind the marble-top bar, experienced shuckers trade jokes with regulars, and from 3pm to 6pm on Tuesdays through Fridays, they also serve $1 oysters to happy customers. Yes, you read that price right.

Munch on Crawfish

CASUAL DINING

MAP: 9 P108 **D6**

Finally, make your way to **Frankie & Johnny's** *(frankieandjohnnys.net)*, another old-school family restaurant. The fried chicken is excellent, but we come here in spring for the crawfish platters, 'berled' (boiled) and spicy. Best shared

THE BIG MUDDY

The Mississippi is no lazy river. An immense volume of water, its sand roils with tremendous, turbulent force, eddying and scouring at the snakelike curves of its banks. The river runs some 2350 miles from Minnesota to the Gulf of Mexico, and its drainage basin extends from the Rockies to the Alleghenies, covering 40% of the continental US. It also moves over 500 million tons of sediment into the Gulf each year, depositing soil and spreading it east and west as the river changes its course. Much of Louisiana, Mississippi and Alabama were created by the Mississippi.

with family, friends and a pitcher of beer for a perfect New Orleans moment.

Wander a Collegiate Campus

UNIVERSITY

MAP: 10 P108 D3

The campus of **Tulane University**, one of the premier private universities of the South, is an attractive tableau of live oaks, red-brick buildings and green quads spread across 110 acres north of Audubon Park (p112). There is a definite vibe here – you might stumble across a protest, or get invited to a keg party – and all in all, it's a pleasant place to stretch your legs.

See Cutting-Edge Works of Art

ART MUSEUM

MAP: 11 P108 D2

The student life that swirls around the campuses of Tulane and Loyola infuses much of Uptown's culture, while some of the on-campus institutions round out the city's more cerebral attractions. Tulane's **Newcomb Art Museum** *(newcombartmuseum.tulane.edu; admission free)* is a great spot to soak up some art, with works from colonial portraiture to engravings by John James Audubon. It's flanked by beautiful, stained-glass triptychs from Tiffany & Co. It's closed Sunday and Monday.

Browse Rare Collections

ARCHIVES

MAP: 12 P108 D2

The **Tulane University Special Collections** include both the **Southeastern Architectural Archive** and the **Hogan Archive of New Orleans Music & New Orleans Jazz** *(library.tulane.edu; admission free)*. The former focuses on different aspects of architecture in the Gulf South (Louisiana to Florida), while the latter comprises rare materials, including 78rpm recordings. The special collections are open to the public from Monday to Friday (during school term only), but researchers

THE CARIBBEAN CONNECTION

Following a 1791 revolt led by enslaved people, thousands of enslavers fled St Domingue (now Haiti) with their 'property' (enslaved human beings) and arrived in Louisiana, bolstering French-speaking Creole traditions. At the same time, thousands of the formerly enslaved also relocated from St Domingue to New Orleans as free people of color. By 1810, some 10,000 of these islanders had arrived in New Orleans, doubling the total population and tripling the population of free people of color. This influx from St Domingue also injected an indelible trace of Caribbean culture (including the practice of voodoo) that remains in evidence to this day.

should make an appointment if they want to access material.

Step Through Leafy Loyola

UNIVERSITY

MAP: 13 P108 **D3**

Next door is **Loyola University**, another private university with more than 4700 students. It opened as a Jesuit college in 1904, and it's another wonderfully scenic campus, with live oaks, beautiful buildings and open quads.

Catch Special Events on Freret

MONTHLY MARKET & FESTIVAL

MAP: 14 P108 **G3**

Freret St is packed with shops, bars, cafes and eateries, all the way from Napoleon to Broadway Ave. In terms of vibe, there are a lot more locals than tourists here, and the strip attracts a certain local type – namely, students and professionals.

You can bank on spending at least two hours wandering around Freret, but if you come on the first Saturday of the month *(11am to 6pm)*, you can lose a day at the **Freret St Market** *(freretmarket.org)*, where vendors hawk local arts, crafts and food. The last Saturday in March is given over to the **Freret St Festival** *(freretstreetfestival.org)*, which turns six blocks into a street party.

Dine & Drink on Freret

RESTAURANTS & BARS

You won't lack for culinary choices on Freret. On just two blocks (from Napoleon Ave to Cadiz St) are two standout restaurants and one excellent coffee shop: the **High Hat Cafe** (MAP: 15 P108 **F3**; *highhatcafe.com*) is famous for its upscaled, tablecloth-worthy executions of New Orleans staples like po'boys and catfish plates. Across the street is the **Bearcat Cafe** (MAP: 16 P108 **G3**; *bearcatcafe.com*), which splits its breakfast menu between vegetarian 'Good Cat' and carnivorous 'Bad Cat' sections.

If you need a drink, don't miss **Cure** (MAP: 17 P108 **F3**; *curenola.com*), one of the first dedicated cocktail bars to open post-Katrina.

Join the Riverbend Revelry

MUSIC VENUES

Some travelers seem to think that the music of New Orleans is exclusively concentrated in the French Quarter or downtown. If you're one of them, head to Uptown and open your ears.

Out in the Riverbend, the **Maple Leaf** (MAP: 18 P108 **B1**; *mapleleafbar.com*) has been packing in crowds seven nights a week since 1974. Given the proximity to Tulane and Loyola, there's a decent student crowd, but everyone enjoys the regular gigs, with mainstays like Grammy-winning pianist Jon Cleary (who was once joined on stage by Bonnie Raitt) and the TBC Brass Band. There's a hole-in-the-wall vibe here, offset by a long concert hall.

Just a few blocks away is **Carrollton Station** (MAP: 19 P108 **C1**;

carrolltonstationnola.com), an ancient gin joint that hosts live music, comedy acts and open mics on a nightly basis.

Follow the Sound to Magazine

MUSIC CLUB

MAP: 20 P108 **F6**

Down on Magazine St, **Le Bon Temps Roule** *(lbtrnola.com)* – usually just called 'The Bon Temps' (pronounced 'Bahn Tahn') has been packing in crowds since 1979. The actual building dates to the 1890s, although it can feel a lot older than that when the crowd starts stomping in time to the Soul Rebels brass band, who call this dive their regular home (on Thursdays). Fridays and Saturdays bring a mixed bag of rock, blues and funk.

Catch a Concert at the Legendary Tipitina's

MUSIC CLUB

MAP: 21 P108 **G6**

Last, but by no means least, is **Tipitina's** *(tipitinas.com)*. Another late 1970s baby (1977, to be exact), 'Tips' is named for a classic jam performed by the great American singer and pianist Professor Longhair. The building that houses Tips has seen previous incarnations as a gym and a brothel, and local radio station WWOZ used to operate upstairs of the main concert hall. They would broadcast shows here by lowering a microphone through a hole cut in the floor.

The Neville Brothers, Phish, Dr John, and Jane's Addiction have also recorded live albums at this legendary venue, following the bright idea of WWOZ. These days, all you gotta do is buy a ticket and enjoy the acts from the ground floor.

See NOLA at its Spookiest

HALLOWEEN DECORATIONS

New Orleans loves Halloween almost as much as it does Mardi Gras: both holidays celebrate consumption, costuming and a general thumbing of the nose at the powers that be. Two of New Orleans' most beloved Halloween institutions can be found on Magazine St and St Charles Avenue. Both are outside viewing only. Down in the Garden District, the **Ghost Manor** (MAP: 22 P108 **H5**; *ghostmanor.org*) is primarily aimed at families – it's a (gently) spooky house that lights up every 20 minutes (on select dates) with an animatronic musical revue complete with dancing skeletons and lip-syncing monsters. In Uptown, the **Skeleton House** (MAP: 23 P108 **D4**; *@skeletonhousenola*), at 6000 St Charles Avenue, is an enormous mansion with even bigger grounds. In October, it gets covered in kooky skeletons bearing groan-worthy pun signs.

Read up on New Orleans in a Stately Mansion

CITY LIBRARY

MAP: 24 P108 **F5**

Poised elegantly above shady stands of palms, the **Milton H Latter Memorial Library** *(nolalibrary.org)* was once a

Le Bon Temps Roule
WILLIAM A. MORGAN/SHUTTERSTOCK

private mansion. The Isaac family – who owned the building from 1907 to 1912 and installed Flemish-style carved woodwork, Dutch murals and French frescoed ceilings – passed the property to aviator Harry Williams and his silent-film-star wife, Marguerite Clark. The next owner was local horse racer Robert S Eddy, followed by Mr and Mrs Harry Latter, who gave the building to the city in 1948. Head inside to peruse books and read periodicals in atmospheric rooms set with chandeliers and old oil paintings (the upstairs – where you'll find the fiction section – is a little more ho-hum). Behind the library, the old carriage house has used books for sale at unbeatable prices *(10am to 2pm Wednesday, Thursday and Saturday).*

Sip Wines on St Charles WINE BAR

MAP: 25 P108 **H4**

If you're looking for a place to relax, sip wine and watch the world go by, **Delachaise** *(@delachaisewinebar)* is a great choice. It's just steps from the St Charles Avenue Streetcar (p110)

PREHISTORIC REPTILES

Elizabeth McDade *(@GatorMuseum)*, cofounder of the **Great American Alligator Museum** *(gatormuseum.com)*, shares insight on Louisiana's favorite reptile:

MAP: 28 P108 **H6**

'There are 26 crocodilian species in the world, and only two of those species are alligators: the American alligator and the smaller Chinese alligator. The species was nearly hunted into extinction in the 1970s, but through strong conservation efforts, alligators have made a comeback. Today, there are some two million in Louisiana. Alligators are fairly vulnerable when they're young. Out in the swamps, they're food for animals like great blue herons and even largemouth bass. But once they reach 3 or 4ft in length, nothing will mess with them.'

line. The small plates are wonderful in an indulgent way, especially the over-the-top grilled-cheese sandwich with house-made apple butter. And everyone lovingly recalls the pommes frites – fried in goose fat.

Bite into Melted Perfection CHEESE-CENTRIC RESTAURANT

MAP: 26 P108 **F5**

Founded by an Englishman obsessed with all the right things (namely, meat and fermented milk products), **St James Cheese Co** *(stjamescheese.com)* is the city's best cheese shop, with a veritable atlas of cheese. From the grilled Gruyère to French ham with brie, the sandwiches all sound enticing; we like the mozzarella with basil pesto and salami.

Run on the Levee GREENWAY

MAP: 27 P108 **A1**

Part of the Mississippi River Trail, the **Levee Path** is a unique public greenway that runs atop – you guessed it – the levee. It follows the curves of the Mississippi River all the way from the Fly behind Audubon Park to Jefferson Parish and beyond. It's a nice spot for walking, jogging or biking, but views of the river are occasionally so-so. Be aware there aren't enough paths connecting the levee to the street below, so if you try to cross off the path, you may get ankle deep in Mississippi mud. Still, it's a good little green space.

See p108 for map of locations

Best Places for...

$ Budget $$ Midrange $$$ Top End

Eating

Ice Cream & Snowballs

Creole Creamery $
29 F5
With imaginative flavors like lavender honey, and pear and ginger sorbet, you can't go wrong at this kid- and adult-loved classic. *noon-10pm*

Lucy Boone $
30 H4
A tiny mom-and-pop ice-cream shop that serves up heavenly perfection. *noon-9:30pm*

Hansen's Sno-Bliz $
31 F6
Open since 1939, this place whips up some of New Orleans' best snow-balls (shaved ice with fla-vored syrup). *noon-6pm Tue-Sun Mar-Oct*

Best Date-Night Restaurants

Clancy's $$$
32 C6
This white-tablecloth neighborhood restaurant embraces the good life – and Creole cuisine. *5pm-9:30pm Tue-Sat, 11:30am-2pm Thu & Fri*

Boucherie $$$
33 C1
The house-cured meats and succulent Southern dishes are lauded citywide, as is the exuberance. *5pm-9:30pm Wed-Sat, 11am-2pm Fri*

Delachaise $$
see 25 H4
Enjoy superb small plates, like an over-the-top grilled cheese sandwich with housemade apple butter. *4pm-1am Mon-Thu, noon-2am Fri-Sun*

Mosquito Supper Club $$$
34 H4
A charming spot with a fairy-lit backyard that's home to creative Cajun cooking. *5:30pm-9:30pm Wed-Sun*

International Eats

Saba $$$
35 D5
Modern Israeli cuisine reflecting the diversity of the Jewish diaspora. *5pm-9pm Sun-Thu, to 10pm Fri & Sat, 10am-2:30pm Sat & Sun*

Mister Mao $$
36 G6
Guests share plates of pan-Asian treats like Kashmiri fried chicken. *5pm-9pm Thu-Tue, to 10pm Fri & Sat, 11am-2pm Sat & Sun*

Avo $$$
37 D5
Modern Italian cuisine, with a focus on regional Sicilian specialities, is served at this romantic restaurant. *5pm-9pm Tue-Sat*

Casual Dining & Picnic Fare

Nomiya $$
38 G6
Ramen is always a good idea, especially here. Opt for the tonkotsu pork broth. *11:30am-9pm Tue-Sun, to 10pm Fri & Sat*

Guy's $
39 E6
A legendary po'boy shop where each sandwich is painstakingly made to order, even when the line is out the door (which

Ms Mae's
WILLIAM A. MORGAN/SHUTTERSTOCK

it often is). *11am-4pm Mon-Sat*

Whole Foods $

40 D6

Once a 'barn' for streetcars that were not in use, Arabella Station houses a gigantic grocery store with lots of prepared food that's ideal for a picnic. *8am-9pm*

Zee's Pizzeria $

see 30 H4

With a reputation for only using the freshest ingredients, it's best to go early to beat the rush. *11:30am-8pm Wed-Thu, to 9pm Fri-Sun*

Drinking

Dive Bars

Snake & Jakes

41 C2

It looks like a bayou bait-shack tarted up for Christmas and engenders questionable behavior: long may 'Snakes' reign. *7pm-5am*

Brothers Three

42 G6

The exterior is bright yellow, but Brothers is a cave inside, filled with locals and a 'delta fridge' to keep the beer cold. *noon-4am*

Ms Mae's

see 7 G6

This legendary hole in the wall is a popular spot for pool, arcade games and local beers served ice-cold on draft. *24hrs*

Carrollton Station

see 19 C1

A neighborhood watering hole filled with all the characters that make New Orleans special. *4pm-3am Mon-Fri, from 11am Sat & Sun*

St Joe's

43 E5

This is a fine neighborhood joint for sitting under moody lights in the backyard while sipping the signature blueberry mojito. *3pm-2am Tue-Sun, 5pm-2am Mon*

Classy Drinking Spots

Columns Hotel

44 H4

With its raised front porch, elegant courtyard and mahogany bar within, the Columns is an atmospheric choice for drinks, small plates or a meal. *11:30am-10pm*

The Chloe

45 G4

Another beauty on St Charles, this boutique hotel has some lovely nooks for drinks – both in the verdant front yard and by the pool out back. *11am-10pm*

Bouligny Tavern

46 H5

Sexy lighting, inventive cocktails and an extensive wine list – it all comes together in a lively, flattering tableau on Magazine St. *4pm-midnight Mon-Sat*

Shopping

Souvenirs & Toys

Dirty Coast

47 D5

Sells clever T-shirts and bumper stickers ('make wetlands, not war') related to local issues and neighborhood happenings. *11am-6pm Mon-Thu, 10am-6pm Fri-Sun*

Magic Box Toys

48 E6

Near the intersection with Octavia St, kids will definitely want to spend time perusing the stuffed racks at this delightful toy store. *10am-5pm Mon-Thu, 10am-6pm Fri-Sat, 11am-4pm Sun*

Music & Records

Peaches Records & Tapes

see 7 G6

This excellent shop does the holy work of promoting, cataloging and marketing the best local music in New Orleans. *10am-7pm Mon-Sat, 10am-5pm Sun*

Uptown Music Exchange

49 E6

Budding or seasoned musicians may want to window shop at this store, where you can buy or trade for new and used instruments. *1pm-6pm Tue-Fri, noon-5pm Sat*

Crafts & Housewares

Potsalot

50 H5

Unique pieces made for use in the kitchen, bathroom and den; find bowls, platters and, yep, lotsa pots. *11am-5pm Tue-Sat*

Hazelnut

51 E5

In addition to classic New Orleans-print toile, there's gilded glassware, postmodern ceramics and other must-haves. *10am-6pm Mon-Sat, noon-5pm Sun*

See p137
for eating
listings

Explore Mid-City, Bayou St John & City Park

Historically located at the bottom of the city's geographical depression in a land of swampy lowlands and hidden gambler dens, today, Mid-City and its adjacent neighborhoods form one of the loveliest residential areas in New Orleans. This semi-amorphous district includes long lines of shotgun houses, bike lanes and clusters of urban life pulsing with restaurants and bars. The Mississippi River may be the defining waterway of New Orleans, but the slow Bayou St John, framed by pretty houses, is what wends through the city proper. The bayou flows into and around the gorgeous green spaces of City Park, the largest green space in the city.

Getting Around

Streetcar

The City Park spur of the Canal St streetcar hits Carrollton St, then heads all the way to the park.

Bus

The 91 runs up Esplanade Ave, turns into Mid-City and drops by City Park. The 27 follows Louisiana Ave and also hits the park. The 94 bus runs along Broad, cutting through Mid-City and the Tremé.

Car

Free street-parking is plentiful throughout these neighborhoods.

Bicycle

You can pedal here via the Lafitte Greenway or Esplanade Ave, which has a bicycle lane.

City Park (p129)
WILLIAM A. MORGAN/SHUTTERSTOCK

★

THE BEST

FLORAL BLOOMS Botanical Gardens (p129)

NATURE ESCAPE Couturie Forest (p130)

ART EXHIBITIONS New Orleans Museum of Art (p131)

BIKE PATH Lafitte Greenway (p133)

MUSIC FESTIVAL Jazz & Heritage Festival (p133)

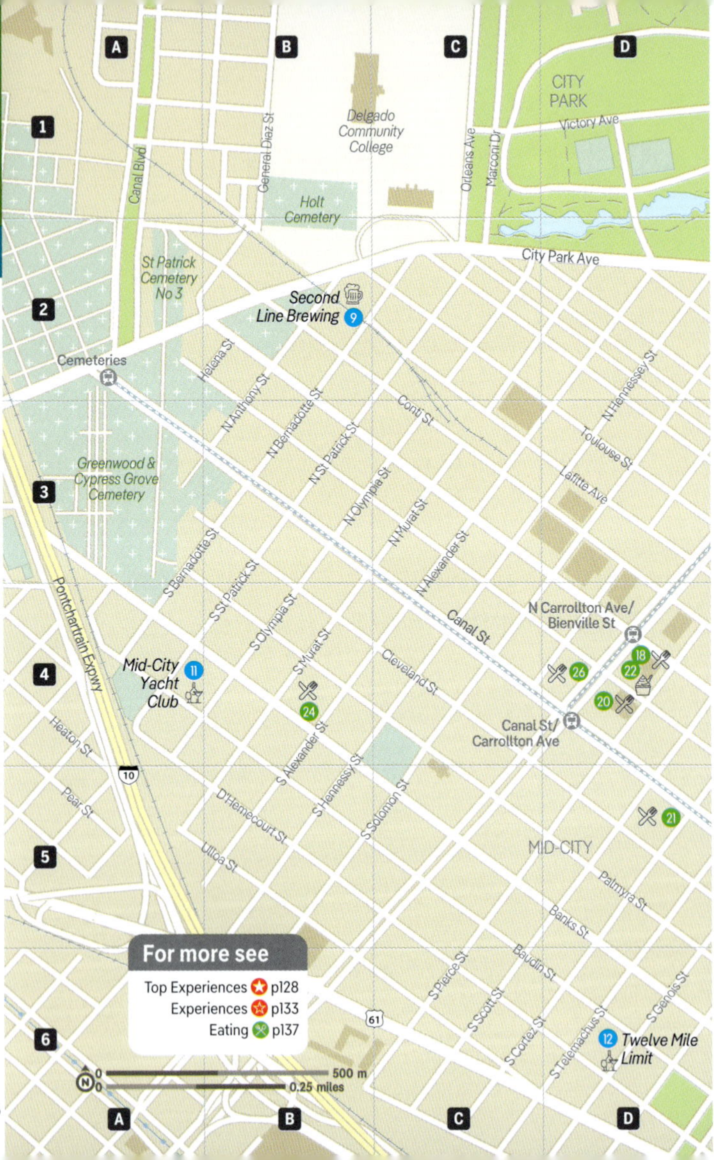

For more see
Top Experiences p128
Experiences p133
Eating p137

EXPLORE

MID-CITY, BAYOU ST JOHN & CITY PARK

★ TOP EXPERIENCE

City Park

Live oaks, Spanish moss and lazy bayous frame the masterpiece of urban planning that is **City Park**. Three miles long and 1 mile wide, dotted with gardens, waterways and bridges, and home to a captivating art museum, the park is bigger than NYC's Central Park, and it's New Orleans' prettiest green space.

MAP P126 **F2**

PLANNING TIP
The Canal streetcar (City Park/Museum Route) is the best way to get to the park. If you're driving, you'll find free parking near the museum and Cafe du Monde.

Scan this QR code for more insights, info & special events.

Historic Oak Grove

City Park's gnarled, aged and stately arboreal life is magnificently visible in the **Historic Oak Grove**, home to strands of thousands of mature live oaks – some as old as 600 years – along with bald cypresses, Southern magnolias and other species. During Hurricane Katrina, nearby canals flooded and inundated more than 90% of the park with up to 8ft of saltwater. Many priceless trees were lost, but the ones here, clustered near City Park Ave, remain.

Peristyle

The eye-catching **Peristyle** pavilion, built in 1907, is marked by Ionic columns and flanked by four lions. It looks like it was summoned from ancient Greece via a time machine. It was originally built for private events and is the site of many weddings and *quinceañera* (traditional celebration of a girl's 15th birthday) photo sessions.

Cafe du Monde

Scratch your beignet itch at the **Cafe du Monde**'s City Park outpost. Here, you can enjoy all that powdered sugar while listening to birds chirp in the trees.

KIT LEONG/SHUTTERSTOCK

Botanical Gardens

One of the park's most popular attractions (and wedding venues), the **Botanical Gardens** *(adult/child $12/6)* are home to both local and international flora. You'll also find stirring examples of Works Progress Administration (WPA) expertise and well-designed pavilions and function halls.

Storyland

There are no rides at **Storyland** *(adult/child 36in & under $6/free)*, but the fairytale statuary provides plenty of fuel for young imaginations. Children can play with the Jabberwocky from *Alice's Adventures in Wonderland* or enter the mouth of the whale from *Pinocchio*. If the characters seem strangely similar to Mardi Gras floats, it's because they were created by master float-builder Blaine Kern.

QUICK BREAK
The best place for a bite or a coffee is at NOMA's **Cafe NOMA**, which you can visit without paying the admission fee.

MUSICAL OAK
The Singing Oak stands festooned with chimes, some up to 14ft in length. For a bit of enchantment, stand beneath the tree during a breeze and listen to the tinkling bells.

Carousel Gardens

The little amusement park of **Carousel Gardens** *(adult/child $15/25)* is anchored by its namesake carousel. It's a gem of vintage carny-ride happiness; the lovingly restored antique is housed in a 1906 structure with a stained-glass cupola – a spectacular, twinkly slice of amusement-park history in its own right.

Couturie Forest

The wildest section of the park is the scad of hardwood trees known as **Couturie Forest**, where live oaks shade leafy underbrush and mushrooms peek out of the moist soil. Park your car in the lot off the Harrison Ave traffic

Carousel Gardens
JAIMIE TUCHMAN/SHUTTERSTOCK

circle or at the City Park volunteer office (1031 Harrison Ave), then take any branching trail and get pleasantly lost. Back amid the trees, you might come upon the daunting peak of Laborde Mountain, the highest point in New Orleans, which towers over the park at a Brobdingnagian 27ft tall. This majestic peak was formed by ancient geologic forces - namely, the leftover debris from the construction of I-610.

Big Lake

It might not be the most imaginative name in the history of park nomenclature, but **Big Lake** is just that: the biggest body of water in City Park. Many locals have spent their days making multiple quiet loops of the paved walking path that circumnavigates the lake. Want to get on the water? Rent a pedal-powered swan boat via **Wheel Fun Rentals** *(wheelfunrentals.com; $38 per hour)*.

Museum of Art

Inside the park, the elegant **New Orleans Museum of Art** *(noma.org; adult/child $20/free)*, aka NOMA, was opened in 1911 and is well worth a visit for its special exhibitions, marble atrium and galleries of African, Asian, Flemish, Italian and American Southern art. Temporary exhibitions have become increasingly innovative over the past few years and may include retrospectives on American furniture design, Ancient Egyptian temple art or galleries that grapple with the city's complicated racial geography. NOMA resembles a sort of Greco Roman temple lording over an alleyway of trees, making for an impressively handsome gateway to the park. It's closed Mondays.

Sculpture Garden

The **Sydney & Walda Besthoff Sculpture Garden** *(admission free)* is located just outside NOMA,

GRAND FOUNTAIN
Popp Fountain is a wonderful design from the 1920s. Promenades planted with perennials and 26 Corinthian columns surround the centerpiece: water erupting from a bronze base of cavorting dolphins.

DUELING GROUND
For years, City Park was a space where dueling men would shoot each other beneath the **Dueling Oak**, today located near the Sculpture Garden.

GATORS!
There are alligators here! If you're walking your dog or near the water, keep an eye out. We're not kidding – local gators aren't common, but they're not unheard of.

PARK HISTORY
The park was established in 1854. Much of the infrastructure and improvements, including the pathways, bridges and art deco flair, were built by the WPA during the Great Depression.

amid a wooded quilt of streams, pathways, lovers' benches and, of course, sculpture – mainly of the contemporary sort. Cleverly engineered waterways accompany the walking paths – a nod to the ubiquitous presence of water in New Orleanian life. During spring and summer, theatrical productions are often put on here.

Children's Museum

The **Louisiana Children's Museum** *(lcm.org; adults & children $18)* is like a high-tech kindergarten where wee ones can play in interactive bliss till nap time. Lots of corporate sponsorship equals lots of hands-on exhibits. The Move with the River gallery offers opportunities for splashy play while kids learn about river systems. Elsewhere, little ones can shop in a pretend grocery store or make leaf rubbings of trees found in City Park. While walk-ins are welcome, the children's museum recommends buying timed-entry tickets before visiting. It's closed Mondays.

EXPERIENCES

Cycle the Greenway

CYCLING & PEDESTRIAN PATH

MAP: 1 P126 **F5**

The **Lafitte Greenway** extends for 2.6 miles from the Tremé (near the intersection of Basin St and Lafitte Ave) up through Mid-City all the way to Carrollton Ave. The Mid-City section of the Greenway takes you past spider-branch trees and long marsh grass that clings to the edges of storm drains. It's all very attractive if you appreciate a fecund, subtropical-jungle-overtakes-the-city vibe.

At Hagan Ave, where the Greenway passes Bayou St John, you'll see two sculptures: the Iris of Memory, a metal flower that illuminates more brightly as visitors approach it, and Turning, a series of metal prayer wheels inlaid with mosaics that depict the creative power of the Mississippi River, whose flow has generated the land the city is built on.

Past here, the Greenway thins out, running past businesses, murals, apartment buildings and a large shopping complex where it hits North Carrollton Ave. Cross this busy road if you're going to City Park (p128), and turn right on Alexander St, which will lead you into the greenery.

Join the Party at Jazz Fest

NOLA'S FESTIVAL

MAP: 2 P126 **H2**

One of the world's most famous music events, the **Jazz & Heritage Fest** *(nojazzfest.com; tickets from $110)* is a mainstay of the city's festive calendar and features a fabled lineup of bands and soloists from a wide range of genres. Local talent adds to the national and international superstars (past luminaries include the Rolling Stones, Elton John, Ed Sheeran and Buddy Guy), and there's also outstanding food, a folklife village, **Second Line Parades** (p144) and kids' activities.

The fest occurs at the Fair Grounds over eight days, with well over a dozen stages scattered around. Some are set up in huge tents where you can take a break from the blazing sun. Other stages overlook large lawns – perfect for setting up a picnic blanket. Food plays a starring role, so come with an appetite to enjoy the jambalaya, gumbo, barbecued oysters and countless other temptations.

The fest runs from Thursday to Sunday over two weekends: the last weekend in April and the first weekend in May.

Watch a Race at the Fair Grounds RACETRACK & FESTIVAL GROUNDS

MAP: 3 P126 **H2**

Most tourists associate the **Fair Grounds** *(fairgroundsracecourse.com)* with the most famous event that kicks off here: the New Orleans Jazz & Heritage Festival (p133). And indeed, during Jazz Fest, the entire neighborhood changes identity, morphing from rainbow residential homes to all-day street parties (along with persistent parking enforcement).

But the Fair Grounds hold their own fascinating legacy. Laid out in 1852, this is the third-oldest race-track in the country. These days, the grounds hold horse races (Louisiana Derby winners of the past are buried in the infield), as well as more idiosyncratic, we're-definitely-in-New-Orleans races: ostrich, dachshund and guys in inflatable T-rex suits. The horse-racing season kicks off around Thanksgiving (fourth Thursday in November) and races are held most weekends through mid-March.

Stroll (or Paddle) to Live Music FESTIVAL

MAP: 4 P126 **F4**

A favorite with locals, **Mid-City Bayou Boogaloo** *(thebayouboogaloo.com; admission from $15)* is a great 'shoulder season' festival that features live music, (usually) pleasant weather and a general sense of conviviality. Folks gather on the green space that runs along Bayou St John – or if they have a boat, in the bayou itself – to chow on crawfish and dig some live music. Louisiana heaven.

Explore Esplanade Avenue SCENIC THOROUGHFARE

It's well worth exploring the portion of **Esplanade Avenue** (MAP: 5 P126 **H3**) that runs between Broad St and City Park. Esplanade follows the 'high ground' of Esplanade Ridge; it's shaded by rows of leafy live oaks and fringed by columned French Creole-style mansions. At 2936 Esplanade, look for the Hindu Temple – dedicated to the Hari Krishna sect – that blends in amid the pastel homes.

JAZZ FESTIN' AROUND MID-CITY

If you're Jazz Festin', make sure to take a break from the Fairgrounds to wander the blocks around Ponce de Leon and Maurepas Sts. It's a friendly scene: folks hang out on porches, entrepreneurial locals sell trays of Jell-O shots, and backyard crawfish boils abound – be nice, and you might get invited to one. There are even impromptu concerts that add to the feeling of joie de vivre, with local performers on hand – proof that New Orleans has a near limitless supply when it comes to musical talent.

Mid-City Bayou Boogaloo
WILLIAM A. MORGAN/SHUTTERSTOCK

The grandest home on Esplanade, Luling Mansion, is actually right off it, on 1436 Leda Ct. It's an 18-room Italianate palace that, in its heyday, sprawled over 30 acres. It's still ridiculously grand and is currently a private residence.

Between Esplanade, Grand Route St John and the wonderfully dubbed Mystery St is **Alcée Fortier Park** (MAP: 6 P126 **H3**), a tiny triangle of land decorated with lights, lanterns and furniture.

Wander an Old Burial Ground

CEMETERY

MAP: 7 P126 **G1**

Nearby is **St Louis Cemetery No 3** *(nolacatholiccemeteries.org)*, one of the city's lesser known (but still magnificent) cemeteries, established in 1854. Of particular note is the striking monument designed by James Gallier Jr (a prominent New Orleans-based architect) to commemorate his mother and father, who were both lost at sea. It's a few steps to the right just after you enter from Esplanade Ave. The cemetery's wrought-iron entrance gate is a beauty.

Relax in Festive Beer Gardens

FAMILY-FRIENDLY BARS

A great little beer garden off the Lafitte Greenway, **Wrong Iron** (MAP: 8 P126 **F4**; *wrongiron.com*) has over 50 beers, plus wines, cocktails and frozen drinks – all on tap. Kids are welcome.

Another Mid-City favorite is **Second Line Brewing** (MAP: 9 P126 **B2**; *secondlinebrewing.com*). The owners have turned a light industrial warehouse into a kicking brewery with a courtyard, kid-friendly play areas and food trucks.

Start the Night in Pal's

NEIGHBORHOOD BAR

MAP: 10 P126 **G4**

Mid-City rarely makes tourists' nightlife lists, which is a little befuddling, as some of the best neighborhood bars in New Orleans are here. Spend a night hopping between some of them; you'll want a cab or rideshare to get around.

Just blocks from Bayou St John, **Pal's** *(@palsloungenola)* is a superlative neighborhood bar. The crowd is diverse in just about every way, meaning all sorts mingle here and often spill out onto the street. You might not expect great cocktails at such an unapologetically divey joint, but mixed drinks like the Gingerita could hold their own in any fancy Manhattan or London mixology joint.

Mingle at the Mid-City Yacht Club

SPORTS BAR

MAP: 11 P126 **A4**

Further north, at the edge of Mid-City, you'll find the **Mid-City Yacht Club** *(midcityyachtclub.com)*, which is nothing like an actual yacht club. This bar earned its name when one of the owners took his boat out to save flooded Katrina victims; the bar itself is made from wood salvaged from storm debris. The vibe is somewhere between a neighborhood watering-hole and a sports bar, and the food is some of the best pub grub around; a burger here is never a bad choice.

Sip with a Fun Crowd

ECLECTIC BAR

MAP: 12 P126 **D6**

Deep in Mid-City, **Twelve Mile Limit** *(twelvemilelimit.com)* is simply a great bar. It's staffed by people who have the skill to work in four-star spots, but who chose to set up shop in this neighborhood, for the neighborhood. The vibe is welcoming, the crowd is young and fun, and the calendar is packed with events like queer dance parties, vinyl record nights, 'sexy' bingo (go on, try it) and karaoke.

See p126 for map of locations

Best Places for...

$ Budget $$ Midrange $$$ Top End

Eating

Cafes & Delis

Bean Gallery $
13 E3
Popular with students and beloved for its airy interior. *6:30am-midnight Sun-Thu, to 10pm Fri & Sat*

Smoke & Honey $$
14 F5
A Jewish deli and Greek restaurant, as well as freshly roasted coffee. *8am-3pm daily, 5-9pm Mon, Tue, Thu-Sat*

Comfort Classics

Liuzza's by the Track $
15 H2
Well known for its gumbo, barbecue shrimp po'boys and deep-fried garlic oysters. *11am-8pm Mon-Fri, to 3pm Sat*

Katie's $$
16 E5
Everything here swims in either remoulade sauce or garlic butter. *11am-9pm Mon-Thu, to 10pm Fri & Sat, 10am-5pm Sun*

Neyow's $$
17 F5
Enjoy reliable blue-chip dishes like breaded pork chops and grilled catfish. *11am-9pm Mon-Thu, to 11pm Fri & Sat, from 10am Sun*

Porgy's $$
18 D4
Excellent local seafood, from boiled crawfish to crab boil. *11am-7pm, til 5pm Sun*

Parkway Tavern $
19 F4
Justifiably known for its enormous po'boys, it also serves up some mean gumbo and jambalaya. *10am-6pm Wed-Sun*

Italian

Venezia $$
20 D4
Straight out of a 1950s' mob movie, with check-ered tablecloths and Chianti-bottle candles. *4pm-10pm Wed-Sat & Mon, noon-9pm Sun*

Mandina's $$
21 D5
A venerated temple of Sicilian Louisiana food, with trout almondine and veal cutlets. *11am-9pm Sun-Thu, to 9:30m Fri & Sat*

Angelo Brocato $
22 D4
Opened in 1905, this is the oldest ice-cream shop in New Orleans. *10am-10pm Tue-Sat, to 9pm Sun*

Terranova's $
23 G2
If you're planning on a picnic, this is the best spot in town for Italian meats and cheeses. *8am-6:30pm Mon-Fri, 9am-3pm Sat*

Carnivore's Dilemma

Bub's Burgers $
24 B4
Retro, family-friendly joint with arcade games and fantastic smash burgers. *11am-10pm Tue-Sun*

Toups' Meatery $$$
25 E3
Looks like a spruced-up hunting lodge. Serves meat and boudin. *5pm-10pm Sun-Thu, to 11pm Fri & Sat, 11am-3pm Mon-Sat, from 10am Sun*

Revel $
26 D4
Great cocktails served alongside chart-topping burgers and Belgian-style fries. *4pm-11pm Tue-Thu, to midnight Fri & Sat*

See p147
for eating and drinking listings

Explore Tremé-Lafitte

It all comes down to the culture, a unique blend of Caribbean, West African and European folkways that tangle together in these homes, streets and churches. To this day, few places hold their finger on New Orleans' cultural pulse like this handful of blocks – arguably the oldest African American neighborhood in the country. This is where jazz was invented by descendants of both free people of color and enslaved people, who mixed African rhythms with European syncopation and homegrown improvisation. When you consider that jazz led to rock led to hip-hop led to pop, just remember, the roots of that musical tree find their soil here.

Getting Around

Bus

The area is well served by city bus lines. The 51, 52, 57 and 91 all pass through Tremé-Lafitte.

Streetcar

The Rampart streetcar runs along the edge of the neighborhood to the corner of St Claude and Elysian Fields Ave.

Bicycle

The Lafitte Greenway begins and ends here. Esplanade Ave has a bicycle lane. Note that smaller residential streets may have serious potholes.

Car

Parking is difficult on Rampart St, but usually not much of an issue within the neighborhood.

Louis Armstrong Park (p145)

JEJIM/SHUTTERSTOCK

★ **THE BEST**

BURIAL GROUND TOUR St Louis Cemetery No 1 (p142)

SUNDAY CELEBRATION Second Line Parades (p144)

CULTURAL INSIGHT Backstreet Cultural Museum (p145)

GREEN SPACE Louis Armstrong Park (p145)

CREOLE CUISINE Dooky Chase (p146)

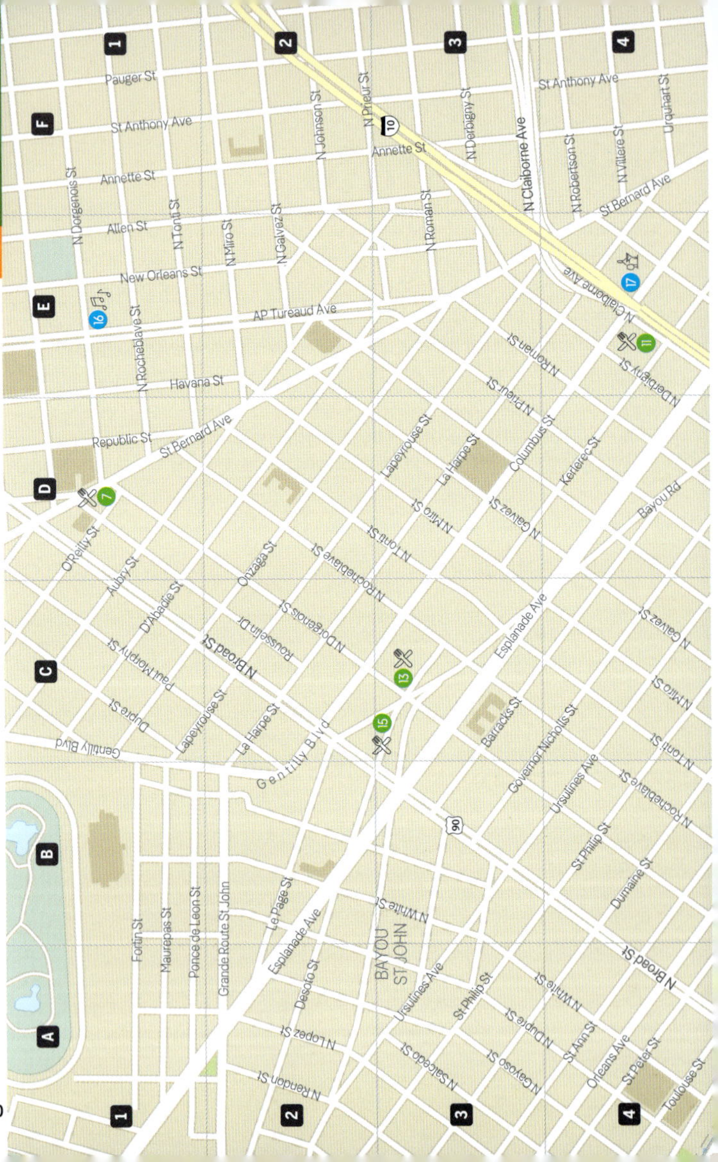
Pauger St
St Anthony Ave
Annette St
Allen St
N Dorgenois St
New Orleans St
N Tonti St
N Miro St
N Galvez St
N Johnson St
N Prieur St
10
N Derbigny St
N Claiborne Ave
N Robertson St
N Villere St
Urquhart St
St Bernard Ave
N Roman St
AP Tureaud Ave
N Rocheblave St
Havana St
Republic St
O'Reilly St
Aubry St
D'Abadie St
Paul Morphy St
Dupre St
Gentilly Blvd
Onzaga St
N Broad St
Lapeyrouse St
La Harpe St
Columbus St
Kerlerec St
Bayou Rd
Esplanade Ave
Barracks St
Governor Nicholls St
Ursulines Ave
St Philip St
Dumaine St
St Ann St
Orleans Ave
St Peter St
Toulouse St
N Dorgenois St
Rousselin Dr
Fortin St
Maurepas St
Ponce de Leon St
Grande Route St John
Le Page St
Desoto St
N Lopez St
N Rendon St
N White St
BAYOU ST JOHN
N Salcedo St
N Gayoso St
N Dupre St
90
16
7
17
11
13
15
A
B
C
D
E
F
1
2
3
4

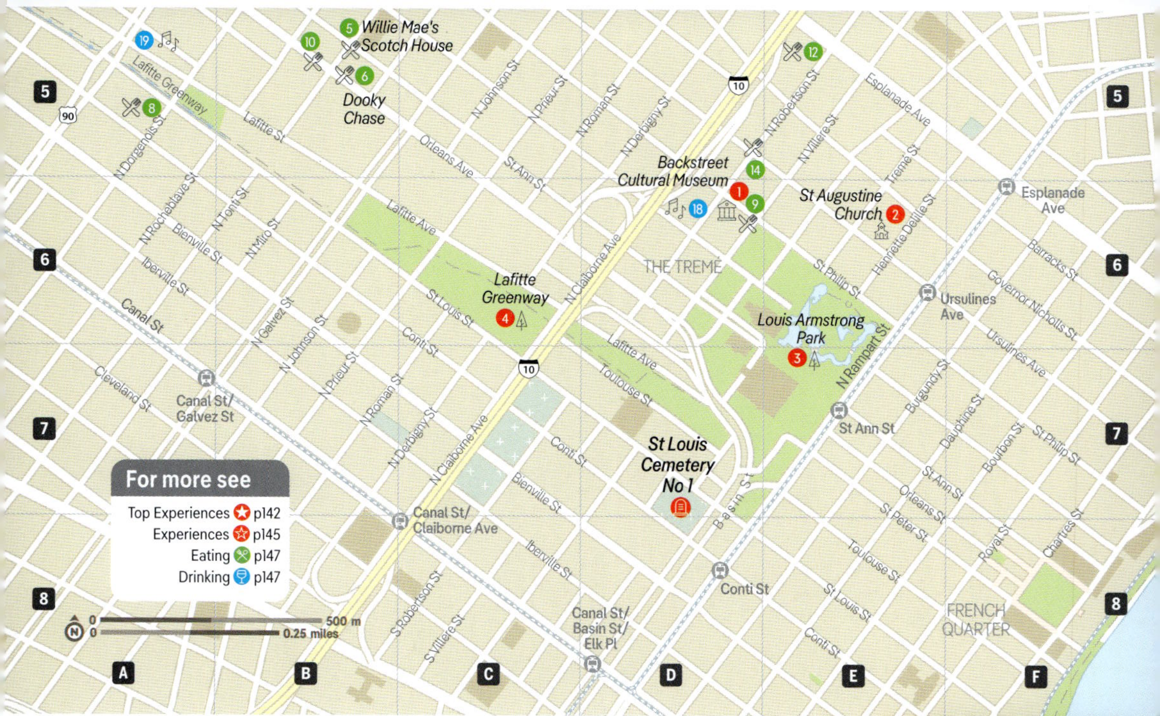
Willie Mae's Scotch House
Dooky Chase
Backstreet Cultural Museum
St Augustine Church
THE TREMÉ
Lafitte Greenway
Louis Armstrong Park
St Louis Cemetery No 1
FRENCH QUARTER
Esplanade Ave
Ursulines Ave
St Ann St
Conti St
Canal St/ Basin St/ Elk Pl
Canal St/ Claiborne Ave
Canal St/ Galvez St
Lafitte Greenway
Lafitte St
Orleans Ave
St Ann St
N Johnson St
N Prieur St
N Roman St
N Derbigny St
N Robertson St
N Villere St
Treme St
Henriette Delille St
Barracks St
Governor Nicholls St
Ursulines Ave
St Philip St
N Rampart St
Burgundy St
Dauphine St
Bourbon St
St Philip St
St Ann St
Orleans St
St Peter St
Toulouse St
St Louis St
Conti St
Royal St
Chartres St
Basin St
Lafitte Ave
Toulouse St
Conti St
Bienville St
Iberville St
N Claiborne Ave
St Louis St
Conti St
N Dorgenois St
N Rocheblave St
N Tonti St
N Miro St
Bienville St
Iberville St
Canal St
N Galvez St
N Johnson St
N Prieur St
N Roman St
N Derbigny St
N Claiborne Ave
Cleveland St
S Robertson St
S Villere St
For more see
Top Experiences p142
Experiences p145
Eating p147
Drinking p147
500 m
0.25 miles
A
B
C
D
E
F
5
6
7
8

★ TOP EXPERIENCE

St Louis Cemetery No 1

New Orleans was historically influenced by the mausoleum-building cultures of the Spanish and French, and large aboveground necropolises are a common sight across town. The most famous is St Louis Cemetery No 1, which opened in 1789. Visits are by authorized guides only.

MAP P140 **D7**

PLANNING TIP
Plan a morning or afternoon tour with Cemetery **Tours NOLA** *(adult/child $25/18)* to avoid the crowds and the heat – which can feel intense amid the shadeless, treeless burial ground.

Scan this QR code to book a tour with Cemetery Tours NOLA.

Basin St Station

The 45-minute tour departs from across the street from the cemetery at Basin St Station *(basinst station.com)*, which is itself an attractive information center with solid exhibits on the city's history and neighborhoods. The building is an architectural icon. Constructed in 1904, this was once the freight and baggage office of the Southern Railway and it's the last vestige of the five railroad stations and vintage buildings that once dotted downtown.

The Tombs

St Louis No 1 is filled with some of the city's most prominent historical figures. Civil-rights figure Homer Plessy rests in the cemetery, as do real-estate speculator Bernard de Marigny (namesake of Faubourg Marigny) and architect Benjamin Henry Latrobe (designer of the central tower of the St Louis Cathedral, among other structures).

The Italian Mutual Benevolent Society tomb is the tallest monument in the cemetery. Like other immigrant groups in New Orleans, the Italians formed a benevolent association to pool funds and assist with burial costs. This tomb was also featured in a controversial scene of the film *Easy Rider*, when Peter Fonda, high on LSD, climbs atop a statue and sits there crying his eyes out. Once the movie came out, the archdiocese banned filming here.

PAGE LIGHT STUDIOS/SHUTTERSTOCK

Marie Laveau

No grave in St Louis No 1 quite holds the attention of the public like the tomb of Marie Laveau, the supposed 'Voodoo Queen of New Orleans.' There is plenty of historical disagreement on the subject; many a voodoo-store employee in the Quarter will argue that Laveau was a sort of witch-cum-Civil-Rights-champion, while some local historians contend she gained her fame by packaging and commercializing voodoo for a gullible, wealthy white audience.

In the past, her crypt was the source of much of the vandalism that has plagued St Louis No 1, when ostensible 'followers' scrawled 'magic Xs' on the tomb. It's a tragic development, as debates over which Marie Laveau – mother or daughter (they shared the name) – was actually buried here show no signs of reaching a resolution.

QUICK BREAK
A short hop from the cemetery, the **Backatown Coffee Parlor** *(8am-3pm)* is a charming, sun-filled cafe where you can linger over lattes, pastries, quiches and sandwiches.

★ TOP EXPERIENCE

Second Line Parades

Second Line refers to New Orleans' wildly celebratory neighborhood parades, especially those put on by the city's African American Social Aid and Pleasure (S&P) clubs. Fast stepping, snazzily dressed S&P members are followed by a band – and everyone else who cares to dance through the city.

PLANNING TIP
Second Lines occur every Sunday of the year from September through May, usually in or around Tremé and Central City. To find the parade route, check out WWOZ's Takin' It to the Streets *(wwoz.org)*.

Scan this QR code for info on upcoming Second Line Parades.

Brilliant Outfits & Brassy Rhythms

It's a dazzling sight, watching S&P members decked out in flash suits, hats and shoes, plus decorated umbrellas and fans, march on a predetermined route through the city in the company of a hired band. There's lots of pumping music and 'steppin' – a kind of syncopated marching dance that looks like soldiers in formation overcome by an uncontrollable need to get funky. This is the First Line.

Joining In

Marching behind the S&P members and the band is the Second Line. These are the crowds that gather to celebrate the music. Hundreds, sometimes thousands, of people dance in the Second Line, stopping for drinks and food along the parade route. Strangers are welcome to join as well – just read the room. If you're going to take photos, don't get in the way of dancers or the band, and remember that Second Lines exist for the local community, not your consumption. A regular Second Line can roll for hours, but you can dip in and out for as long or little as you please. Come with a flexible schedule; things don't always start on time.

EXPERIENCES

Learn about Deep-Rooted Traditions
AFRICAN-AMERICAN HERITAGE

MAP: 1 P140 **D6**

The unique culture of New Orleans is deeply rooted in African American folkways, traditions and music, all of which took on a distinct character in south Louisiana. Start your visit at the **Backstreet Cultural Museum** *(backstreet museum.org; adult/child $25/10)* on St Philip St. Mardi Gras Indian suits grab the spotlight with dazzling flair – and finely crafted detail – in this informative space, which examines many of the distinctive elements of African American culture in New Orleans.

The museum isn't terribly big, but if you have any interest in the suits and rituals of Mardi Gras Indians, as well as Second Line Parades, Social Aid & Pleasure Clubs (the local African American community's version of civic associations), or organizations like the North Side Skull & Bones, then you should stop by. You're welcome to explore on your own, but the admission fee covers tours that help to place the exhibits in context.

Say a Prayer in St Aug's
CHURCH

MAP: 2 P140 **E6**

Open since 1841, **St Augustine Church** *(staugchurch.org)* is the oldest African American Catholic church in the country, and in some ways, it looks the part. We mean that in a good way: there is a sense of age, tradition and community here, all befitting the main house of worship in the Tremé.

Since its founding, St Augustine has been a place where Creoles, émigrés from St Domingue and free persons of color could worship shoulder to shoulder, even as separate pews were designated for enslaved people. In fact, in 1842, a bidding war between white and free people of color congregants ended with the free people of color claiming ownership of interior pews (one of which was still given over to white congregants), while simultaneously reserving outer pews for enslaved Black worshippers.

Mass is held at St Augustine at 10am on Sunday and 5pm on Wednesday.

Relax in Louis Armstrong Park
LEAFY PARK

MAP: 3 P140 **E7**

The entrance to massive **Louis Armstrong Park** has to be one of the greatest gateways in the South, a picturesque arch that rightfully ought to be the star set-piece in a period drama about Jazz Age New Orleans.

If City Park is where the city gets active outdoors, Armstrong embodies the sounds of the city, landscaped into a public space. Small festivals kick off here throughout the year *(events.jazzandheritage.org)*, while musicians and the crowds that love them gather under the Louis Armstrong statue or the bust of Sidney Bechet.

ARMSTRONG PARK FESTIVALS

Armstrong Park is the site of three mid-sized festivals put on by the **New Orleans Jazz & Heritage Foundation** *(jazzandheritage.org)*.

Congo Square Rhythms Festival is held in late March and celebrates all layers of New Orleans Black culture, from Second Lines to Mardi Gras Indians to jazz to bounce.

Louisiana Cajun Zydeco Festival is where you'll catch zydeco (a genre that blends Creole, R&B and blues) on the last weekend of May.

Tremé Creole Gumbo Festival celebrates the Tremé, its music and its culinary legacy via a family-friendly weekend party, held in early November.

Explore the Lafitte Greenway

PARK

MAP: 4 P140 **C6**

The 2.6-mile **Lafitte Greenway** is a linear park that connects the Tremé to City Park via Bayou St John, traversing the length of the Tremé and Mid-City along the way. It's a bicycle- and pedestrian-friendly trail that follows the course of one of the city's oldest transportation paths. It was originally a canal and later a railroad. For more on the Greenway, see p133.

Eat NOLA's Best Fried Chicken

RESTAURANT

MAP: 5 P140 **B5**

When it comes to fried bird, no one in town can touch the legendary **Willie Mae's Scotch House** *(williemaesscotchhouse.com)*. Originally opened in 1957 by Willie Mae Seaton, the Scotch House, like many businesses of the time, wore many hats: restaurant, barber and bar (hence 'Scotch House'). Eventually it became a dedicated eatery, thanks to the strength of its signature fried chicken, which has been dubbed the best in the world by the James Beard Foundation, among others. In this case, the hype isn't far off – it's superlative fried bird. Willie Mae's was damaged by fire in 2023, but is projected to reopen by the time you read this.

Indulge in Creole Cooking

RESTAURANT

MAP: 6 P140 **B5**

If you've ever seen Disney's *The Princess & the Frog*, you have, in a small way, been to **Dooky Chase's** *(dookychaserestaurants.com)*. The character Tiana was based on the queen of New Orleans Creole cuisine, Leah Chase, who more or less ran the restaurant for seven decades. The vegetarian gumbo z'herbes, served on Thursday during Lent, is the great New Orleans dish, done with mustard greens, beet tops, spinach, kale, collards and Leah knows what else; committed carnivores should give it a try.

Best Places for...

See p140 for map of locations

$ Budget $$ Midrange $$$ Top End

Eating

Breakfast Spots & Cafes

Buttermilk Drop Bakery $

7 D1

Beignets have nothing on buttermilk drops, aka doughnut holes filled with lots of butter. *6am-5pm Mon-Sat, to 4pm Sun*

Flour Moon Bagels $

8 A5

Enjoy a rosemary and salt bagel or a beautifully baked *bialy* (bagel-type roll topped with carmelized onions). *Hours vary*

Tremé Coffeehouse $

9 D6

The sort of cafe every neighborhood deserves: good coffee, sandwiches, a space for local business-people and artists, and laid-back vibes. *7am-5pm Tue-Fri, 8am-2pm Sat & Sun*

Cajun & Creole Cooking

Gabrielle $$$

10 B5

This little cottage doles out rich Cajun plates of braised rabbit, slow-roasted duck and other favorites. *5pm-10pm Wed-Sat*

Cajun Seafood $

11 E4

Head to this takeout stand for seafood and hot plates, including fish platters. *10:30am-8:30pm Mon-Sat, from 11am Sun*

Lil' Dizzy's $

12 E5

Join the crowds at this legendary lunchtime Creole buffet on the corner of Claiborne. *11am-3pm Mon-Sat*

International Flavors

Pagoda Cafe $

13 C3

Serves cafe fare with a global spin, such as mushroom turnovers, mango lassis and guava puff-pastries. *7am-1pm Tue-Sun*

Fatma's Cozy Corner $

14 D5

Fatma's serves Mediterranean cafe fare: paninis, falafel, chicken salad sandwiches and the like. *7:30am-3pm*

Addis Nola $$

15 C3

Ethiopian *tibs* and *wort* (thick stews) scooped up with spongy *injera* flatbread. *noon-10pm Wed-Fri & Mon, from 11am Sat & Sun*

Drinking

Live Music

Bullet's

16 E1

At this sports and live-music joint, the crowd is friendly, the beer is cold, the drinks are strong and the music is good. *10am-11pm*

Kermit's Tremé Mother-in-Law Lounge

17 E4

Owned by iconic trumpeter Kermit Ruffins (who often plays here), this wonderfully odd bar is a Tremé standby and a a prime live-music spot. *4pm-11pm*

Candlelight Lounge

18 D6

This classic but hit-or-miss Tremé dive can sometimes stage great bands. On some nights the music infuses the place and everything is magic. *3pm-1am Thu-Tue*

The Broadside

19 A5

Catch live music jams – some are all-ages, so family friendly – at this laid-back outdoor spot on Broad Ave. *hours vary*

★ WORTH A TRIP

Natchez

The southwestern Mississippi town of Natchez contains an impressive collection of well-preserved 19th-century architecture. Its quiet streets are dotted with elaborate buildings, especially the mighty St Mary Basilica, and historic plantation museums provide insight into the lives of its past residents – both free and enslaved – and the town's relationship with slavery.

PLANNING TIP
You'll need a car to get to Natchez, which is about a three-hour drive from New Orleans. Plan to get an early start (before 8am) or mid-morning (after 10am) to beat the madhouse, rush-hour atmosphere on the interstate.

Scan this QR Code for the Natchez Civil War Sites Driving Tour.

Exploring History

Today, most Natchez plantation estates host tours or operate as guesthouses. although many don't do enough to contextualize the conditions of the enslaved. The **Natchez National Historical Park** aims to give a more holistic perspective on things, with several sites, including **Melrose Estate** *(nps.gov/natc; guided tours $10)*, where the guides balance the lives of the plantation-owning McCurran family with those of the enslaved people who worked there. The National Park Service also administers the **William Johnson House** *(admission free)*, where exhibits tell the story of the life and murder of a free man of color.

Deeper Insight into Culture & History

For more context, visit the small **Natchez Museum of African American Culture & History** *(visit napac.net; by donation)*. It provides a deeper perspective on life during and after slavery, with exhibits on the tragic Rhythm Nightclub fire and local luminaries such as acclaimed writer Richard Wright.

A Gothic Cathedral in Mississippi

The longest-operating Catholic building in Mississippi, **St Mary Basilica** celebrated its first Mass on December 25, 1843. The striking Gothic Revival church has an ornate sanctuary with a soaring, deep-blue ceiling, prominent stained-glass windows, Carrara marble altars and delicate statuary. Self-guided tour pamphlets are inside.

★ WORTH A TRIP

Plantation Tours

One of the most popular day-trips from New Orleans is a tour of the plantation homes along the Mississippi River. It's important to remember that these grand mansions were built on the backbreaking labor of slavery – a big part of the story on some of the tours.

Whitney Plantation

The excellent **Whitney Plantation** *(whitneyplantation.org; guided tour adult/child $32/18, self-guided tour $25/11)* rewrites the plantation script with 1½- to 2-hour guided tours that focus on the lives of the enslaved. It isn't easy history to hear, but the guides do a wonderful job – many of them locals whose ancestors may have worked on the plantation. Guided tours are offered Wednesday to Monday at 10:45am, 12:45pm and 2:15pm. Self-guided tours with an audio device or app are available from 9:30am to 3pm.

Laura Plantation

Another 10-minutes' drive up the road, the **Laura Plantation** *(lauraplantation.com; adult/teen/child $28/20/15)* also does a remarkable job of contextualizing the life of both the free and enslaved on the Duparc Sugar Plantation. Guides rely on historical records and the first-hand accounts of Laura Locoul, a Creole woman who grew up here. Guided tours, available in English and French, last 75 minutes and run every 20 to 40 minutes from 10am to 3:20pm.

Oak Alley Plantation

The most impressive aspect of **Oak Alley Plantation** *(oakalleyplantation.org; adult/child $32/11)* is its canopy of 28 majestic live oaks that line the entry to the grandiose Greek Revival home. The cinematic backdrop has been featured in numerous films, including *Interview with the Vampire.*

PLANNING TIP

You'll need a car to visit these places, which are all within a 75-minute drive of New Orleans. Dining options are limited. One standout is B&C Seafood near Laura Plantation.

Scan this QR code to book a tour of the Whitney Plantation.

★ WORTH A TRIP

Lafayette

Lafayette has fascinating sites dedicated to Cajun history and culture, within a 2½-hour drive of New Orleans. The mid-sized city (population 122,000) is also a great place to indulge in Cajun cooking, with one-of-a-kind seafood and meat delicacies. You're also sure to hear music – a big part of Cajun identity.

PLANNING TIP
Be sure to take a stroll around Lafayette's small, walkable downtown. Jefferson St, located between Cypress St and Vermillion St, is dotted with shops, cafes and restaurants.

Learn about Cajuns & Creoles

The words Cajun and Creole get thrown around a lot in Louisiana, but who are these people? The best place to learn about these rich cultures, in addition to southwestern Louisiana's Native American inhabitants, is at **Vermilionville** *(adults/child $10/6)* in Lafayette.

This recreated 19th-century Cajun village is filled with wooden houses that wind along the bayou. Knowledgeable staff in period garb spin wool and hammer metal to teach visitors about local history. An especially impactful exhibit is the classroom where 'I will not speak French' is written dozens of times on the chalkboard – for decades, French was banned in public schools. There's plenty to read and an excellent restaurant if you're hungry. Check the calendar for live music on weekends.

Take a Food Tour

No one knows traditional cooking better than Marie Ducote-Comeaux of **Cajun Food Tours** *(cajunfoodtours.com; adult/child $65/39)*. Hop in the 14-passenger bus with this proud Cajun and allow her to drive you to five of the best stops in Lafayette for authentic Cajun and Creole eats. On the three-hour tour, you'll try boudin (Cajun sausage), gumbo (seafood or meat stew), po'boys and crawfish.

Scan this QR Code for more info on Vermilionville.

★ WORTH A TRIP

Breaux Bridge & Lake Martin

The tiny town of Breaux Bridge makes a great introduction to Cajun Country, with down-home eateries and music joints amid old-fashioned storefronts. Five miles south of Breaux Bridge, the mossy green waters of Lake Martin set the stage for a memorable swamp tour.

Dance for Your Breakfast

Breaux Bridge is famous for its Saturday morning zydeco breakfasts at **Buck & Johnny's** *(buckandjohnnys.com; $10)*. The Cajun-meets-Italian restaurant has a dining hall that vibrates with zippy zydeco (a genre that blends Creole, R&B and blues) from 8:30am to 11:30am. It's an uproarious time as young and old bob and spin on the dance floor – the $10 extra cover charge for those bottomless mimosas certainly helps. If you can't make it on Saturday, Buck & Johnny's also has live music from around 6pm to 9pm on Thursdays, Fridays and Saturdays.

Look for Wildlife on a Swamp Tour

Touring the swamps and bayous ('streams' in the Choctaw language), on the lookout for alligators and bald eagles, is a bucket-list experience. Recommended outfitters such as **Cajun Country Swamp Tours** *(cajuncountryswamptours.com; $25)* will take you on a two-hour boat excursion to see alligators, yellow-crowned herons and other wetland wildlife on Lake Martin.

If you prefer to get a bit of a workout while you sightsee, the same outfit also rents canoes and kayaks *($20 per person; $20 per hour)*. You can paddle your way across mirror-like waters and stop in secluded spots where you'll hear nothing but the sound of the birds.

PLANNING TIP
Breaux Bridge is liveliest on weekends. Get an early start to make the 2¼-hour drive to the Saturday morning jam session at **Buck & Johnny's**.

Scan this QR Code to book a tour with Cajun Country Swamp Tours.

CITY OF NEW ORLEANS
PORT OF NEW ORLEANS, LA
NEW ORLEANS

New Orleans Toolkit

Steamboat on the Mississippi River **(p44)**

TRAVELVIEW/SHUTTERSTOCK

Family Travel

Outsiders might tell you to leave the kids at home, but there is plenty of fun for the younger set, from streetcar rides to parks, plus loads of activities designed specifically for kids.

Mardi Gras for Families

When it's parade time, many families set up on St Charles Avenue. Kids are placed high up on 'ladder seats' so they can get an adult-height view of the proceedings and catch throws from the floats. These prizes can include shiny doubloons, stuffed animals and myriad light-up toys (swords, rings, necklaces, sunglasses).

CITY PARK

New Orleans' largest park, **City Park**, has loads of family attractions, including a hands-on kids' museum, beignets, playgrounds, swan boats for pedaling around a lake, a small amusement park and lazy waterways filled with fish. Scan this QR code for more insights and info.

Streetcar Adventures

NOLA's various streetcar lines offer a great way to see the city. These vintage trams have a delightful interior of old wooden seats and oversized windows to catch a breeze. Good itineraries include taking the St Charles line to **Audubon Park** or the Canal St Line to **City Park** (p154). Fares are $1.25/0.50 for adults/kids.

Discounted Admission

Kids get free admission to the **New Orleans Museum of Art** and discounted admission at most sites, including the **National WWII Museum**.

Stroller Wars

New Orleans' ill-maintained sidewalks are hard on strollers – you'll want to bring one that is maneuverable and durable.

Meal Planning

Great snacks are always near at hand. Beignets (fried pastries dusted with powdered sugar) make perfect morning treats, while snow cones (crushed ice with flavored syrups) are perfect on hot days. At restaurants, go early (5pm) to avoid crowds.

NINA ALIZADA/SHUTTERSTOCK , BRENT HOFACKER/SHUTTERSTOCK

Accommodations

The city's accommodation options are many, with historic guesthouses in the French Quarter, B&Bs in the Garden District and boutique hotels in the CBD.

Where to Stay if You Love...

History, Architecture & Nightlife

French Quarter (p37) Stay in a boutique guest-house or luxe hotel while exploring all the Quarter has to offer, from restaurants, museums, shops and galleries to late-night revelry.

Museums, Galleries & a Central Location

CBD & Warehouse District (p73) The mostly high-end hotels (some with pools and rooftop bars) make a great base for exploring the local gallery and museum scene.

Leafy Streets, Grand Architecture & Indie Boutiques

Garden District, Lower Garden & Central City (p91) The charming B&Bs – many set in historic homes – provide access to prime shopping along Magazine Street.

Grand Mansions & Scenic Parks

Uptown & Riverbend (p107) Posh hotels and smaller guesthouses offer beauty and tranquility. There's also great dining and shopping, as well as worthwhile nightlife.

Culture & African American Rhythms

Tremé-Lafitte (p139) The main accommodations in this historic part of the city consists of smaller B&Bs with personalized service and effortless charm.

OUR PICK

We Love to Stay in...

The Marigny & Bywater (p57) You'll get a more neighborhood feel in the independently owned guesthouses and B&Bs of this highly walkable area. As well as charming cafes, creative shops and antique stores, you'll find unique restaurants and bars, plus the live music scene of Frenchmen Street. You're also within easy reach of the French Quarter.

HOW MUCH FOR A NIGHT IN A

Boutique hotel **from $350**

B&B **$150–230**

Hostel dorm bed **from $35**

Food, Drink & Nightlife

Allergies & Intolerances

Staff in most restaurants in New Orleans are fairly accustomed to allergies and intolerances. Some menus will explicitly state whether a dish has shellfish, gluten, nuts or other problematic ingredients, but it's always best to confirm with staff before ordering. Vegetarians and vegans should be particularly vigilant, as some seemingly benign dishes might contain animal products.

CRAFTY CREATIVITY

The beer makers of New Orleans love to experiment, and you might come upon mango wheat ales, blueberry Weiss (wheat beer), hibiscus and lime summer ales, and daring sour beers.

PO'BOYS

This overstuffed sandwich is served on local French bread (more chewy, less crispy) and is simply dripping with fillings; the most popular are roast beef, fried shrimp or fried oysters. When you order, your server will ask if you want it 'dressed' with mayonnaise, shredded lettuce and tomato; say yes – it's the obvious way to go.

KCLINE/GETTY IMAGES

Cajun vs Creole Cooking

Cajun and Creole cuisine are different, although both tend to share a love of rich flavors and colorful presentation. Creole is the food of New Orleans and features complex ingredients (seen in remoulade sauce), while Cajun cuisine is 'country' cooking; it's more pork-centric and rarer to find in the city.

HOW TO... Pay the Bill

At cafes and casual dining spots, you'll typically place your order and pay at the counter – and give a tip. (It's common practice to tip, even for counter service.) Tell the server your name (or receive a number) and grab a table while you wait for your food to arrive.

At sit-down spots, you'll receive your check when you ask for it. Tipping is not optional, as servers rely on tips to earn a living wage. The standard tip is 18–20% of the total bill. Most restaurants can split the bill, but be sure to ask before your server rings it up.

PRICE RANGES

The following price ranges refer to the average cost of a main course:

$ under $15
$$ $15-25
$$$ over $25

OPENING HOURS

Cafes 7am-6pm
Restaurants 11am-10pm
Craft breweries 4-11pm Mon-Thu, noon-11pm Fri-Sun

Going Out

Nightlife is integral to New Orleans, and the city knows how to have a good time without a lot of pretension. New Orleanians aren't fans of velvet ropes or mega clubs: things here are much more low-key, with an emphasis on live music rather than DJs, and all are welcome to join in the fun.

Frenchmen Street This area can get aggressively crowded on weekends. But it still hosts the best concentration of music gigs in the city. Music tends to start from around 6pm and continue until 1am; weeknights are a little more casual.

Bourbon Street Despite wall-to-wall tourists, there are a few classic spots here (try **Pat O'Brien's**). Elsewhere in the Quarter, you'll find plenty of variety, from crafty cocktail dens to dingy dive bars. Speaking of dives, locals have a soft spot for these lively gathering dens. Cheap drinks, friendly barkeeps and garrulous regulars generally keep these places humming along.

HOW MUCH FOR A

Café au lait
$3-5

Po'boy
$10-16

Half-dozen chargrilled oysters
$18

High-end jazz brunch
$38-55

Lunch
$15-25

Dinner
$20-38

Beer
$6-10

Cocktail
$10-18

SUZANNE C. GRIM/SHUTTERSTOCK

LGBTIQ+ Travelers

New Orleans has always had a great reputation for diversity, and it remains one of the oldest LGBTIQ-friendly cities in the Western hemisphere.

The Heart of LGBTIQ+ NOLA

Much of the action is in the French Quarter, on and around **Bourbon Street** (p157) – near St Anne. This marks the beginning of the so-called Lavender Line, with a dense concentration of LGBTIQ+ bars, lounges and nightclubs. Highlights here range from historic gems like **Lafitte's** (where Truman Capote and Tennessee Williams used to hang out) to dance-loving party spots like **Oz**.

The Quarter is also the epicenter of Gay Pride New Orleans (June), with a range of parties, art exhibitions and walking tours. The biggest celebrations happen around **Pride Weekend** (p51), usually held early in the month. The festive march kicks off on Saturday and winds from the Marigny through the French Quarter. While the main events can get a little rowdy, there are more family-friendly gatherings during Pride (like Equality Day at Longvue House and Gardens), which attests to the more inclusive nature of New Orleans Pride.

GRRL SPOT

New Orleans' best lesbian party has no fixed address; it pops up once a month for an outrageously fun night of dancing and revelry. Check social media for the latest. Past venues have included **Tipitina's**, **Siberia** and **Cafe Istanbul**.

OUR PICKS

Southern Decadence

If you're out for a wild party, plan for **Southern Decadence**. Held around Labor Day weekend (early September), it's a mix of Gay Pride and Mardi Gras with a more free-spirited feel, and it culminates in street parties and club nights.

SCOTT COLESBY/SHUTTERSTOCK

LGBTIQ+ LISTINGS

Scan this QR code for a comprehensive collection of LGBTIQ+ listings.

LGBTIQ+ Resources

• **gaynola.com** has the best info for what's on when you're in town: leather gatherings, pool parties, drag shows, trivia parties, karaoke and more • **neworleans.gaycities.com** has listings, reviews and LGBTIQ-related content • **ambushmag.com** for a local take on LGBTIQ+ news and issues, have a read of Ambush magazine

Health & Safe Travel

Crime, poor infrastructure and the threat of hurricanes are all important things to keep in mind when traveling to New Orleans.

HURRICANES

Hurricane season runs from June until November. The most active period tends to be in August and September, when powerful winds and heavy rains can cause devastation. If you're in New Orleans and a storm is on the way, follow all official directives.

Minimizing Risk

New Orleans has a high crime rate. While the majority of violent crime occurs between people who already know each other, muggings and carjackings occur across the city. At night, stick to well-traveled areas and avoid deserted streets, especially if you're traveling by yourself. Drink spikings do occur, so don't leave your drink unattended. And keep an eye on your belongings – pickpocketing is all too common in busy bars and clubs, especially on Bourbon Street.

City Alerts

Nola Ready *(ready.nola.gov)* keeps tabs on dangerous weather, excessive heat and polluted tap water.

Cannabis Laws

Although widely used, cannabis products are illegal in Louisiana when used as a recreational drug. Medical cannabis is legal, but it's difficult to get approval if you're just passing through, and out-of-state medical cannabis cards are not accepted. Recreational possession of up to 14 grams is decriminalized and punishable by a fine of up to $100.

INSURANCE

Foreign travelers should seriously consider purchasing travel insurance before visiting the US, as the cost of healthcare can be prohibitive.

QUICK INFO

Drivers
Watch out when crossing the street. Crosswalks are ignored, and (sometimes) red lights, too.

Drinking Safety
Keep an eye on your drink; spikings occur.

Pickpocketing
Be wary in busy bars and clubs.

Responsible Travel

Follow these tips to leave a lighter footprint, support local and have a positive impact on communities.

Tip the Musicians

Decades ago, bar owners on Bourbon and Frenchmen Sts realized they could make more money by offering free live music than by charging a cover. Musicians are paid by the bar, but in practical terms it's never enough to amount to a living wage. Tips are absolutely essential to their livelihood. How much to tip? Add a few dollars if making a short stop, or $5 or more if you're sticking around awhile.

Sustainable Fashion

Shop for recycled fashions at one of New Orleans' many thrift shops. **Magazine Street**, and especially **Funky Monkey**, is prime terrain for one-of-a-kind vintage wear.

OUR PICK

Our Pick: Socially Minded Dining

Support a worthy social enterprise while indulging in old-school home-cooking at **Café Reconcile**. This Central City spot recruits and trains at-risk youth.

Rebuilding Coastline

The Coalition to Restore Coastal Louisiana (CRCL; *crcl.org*) uses discarded oyster shells to rebuild the state's eroding coastline. More than 8000ft of shoreline has been created. Do your part by eating oysters at participating restaurants. Or if you want to get more involved, check CRCL's website for volunteering opportunities, including tree planting and helping out on oyster boats.

Resources

- **neworleans.com/plan/sustainability** a green guide to visiting New Orleans
- **bluebikesnola.com** local bike rentals organized through the city's bike-share program
- **happycow.net** top source for vegetarian and vegan eateries

GREEN ADVENTURES

Consider taking a low-impact tour in the wetlands rather than noisy motorboat or airboat excursions. Kayaking is more immersive, with fewer crowds and more opportunities to experience wildlife.

Get on Your Bike

Cycling is great way to explore New Orleans: the city's size and flat terrain make for easy pedaling. You can rent a bike for the day or hop on a Blue Bike; there are also numerous bike tours. If you're out for more adventure, you'll find some great rides heading out of town. The vehicle-free Mississippi River Trail runs for more than 25 miles from the Fly – just south of **Audubon Park** (p154) to the Bonnet Carré Spillway. Nola Complete Streets Coalition *(nolacompletestreets.org)* has up-to-date maps of bike lanes.

ECO-FRIENDLY CAR RENTALS

If you're renting a car during your stay, consider going electric. You'll find EV charging stations at some hotels and at various points around New Orleans, and your battery will last you in this compact city. Find charging stations at *chargehub.com*.

Climate Change & Travel

It's impossible to ignore the impact we have when traveling; Lonely Planet urges all travelers to engage with their travel carbon footprint, which will mainly come from air travel. While there often isn't an alternative, travelers can look to minimize the number of flights they take, opt for newer aircraft and use cleaner ground transport, such as trains. One proposed solution – purchasing carbon offsets – unfortunately does not cancel out the impact of individual flights. While most destinations will depend on air travel for the foreseeable future, for now, pursuing ground-based travel where possible is the best course of action.

The **UN Carbon Offset Calculator** shows how flying impacts a household's emissions

The **ICAO's carbon emissions calculator** allows visitors to analyze the CO2 generated by point-to-point journeys

CLOCKWISE FROM TOP: MILLAF/SHUTTERSTOCK, CCPIXX PHOTOGRAPHY/SHUTTERSTOCK, TALE/SHUTTERSTOCK

Accessible Travel

Public Transport

All buses are accessible, as are several trams, and the ferry. Download the Le Pass app to plan your trip across town, and tick the option showing accessible routes. The official site of the New Orleans Regional Transit Authority *(norta.com)* has info on riding streetcars, buses and ferries for people with disabilities.

Accommodations

Newer hotels adhere to standards in the Americans with Disabilities Act (ADA) by providing ramps, elevators and accessible bathrooms. B&Bs and older guesthouses generally aren't very accessible. You'll find the best options by focusing your search on modern options in the CBD.

CITY PARK

City Park (p154) has many accessible attractions, including the **New Orleans Museum of Art** (p154), the **Sculpture Garden** and the **Botanical Gardens**. Get there via the accessible streetcar up Canal.

French Quarter

Plan a day in the Quarter by visiting accessible spots such as **St Louis Cathedral**, the **Cabildo** and the **Presbytère**; snacking at **Cafe du Monde**; browsing the **French Market**; and dining at **Arnaud's** or **GW Fins**.

OUR PICK

The **National WWII Museum** (p154) is an outstanding destination for travelers with accessibility needs. All galleries, restrooms and special programs are fully accessible to all visitors. Exhibit videos have captioning in English, and tours for blind/low-vision visitors are available upon request. Complimentary manual wheelchairs are also available. On the last Saturday of the month, the museum offers Sensory Friendly Mornings for individuals of all ages with special needs (and their families).

NIGHTLIFE

These places deserve special mention for being fully accessible: **Carousel Bar**, **NOLA Brewing** and **Hot Tin**. Many other places – like **Tipitina's** (p158) and **Second Line Brewing** – are partially accessible.

Resources

- **wheelchairtravel.org/new-orleans** wheelchair-accessible guide to New Orleans
- **neworleans.com/plan/accessibility** official city-sponsored guide
- **nolarolla.com** handy accessible insights from a New Orleanian

Nuts & Bolts

Opening Hours

Banks 9am-5pm Monday to Thursday, 10am-5:30pm Friday; some branches are open 9am-noon Saturday

Bars Usually 5pm-2am Monday to Thursday and to 4am Friday and Saturday; some bars stay open for 24 hours, while others keep indefinite hours but close if business is slow

Post offices 8:30am-4:30pm Monday to Friday and 8:30am-noon Saturday

Restaurants 11am-11pm (sometimes with a break from 2-5pm); usually closed Sunday and/or Monday

Stores 10am-7pm

QUICK INFO

Time zone Central Time (GMT/UTC minus six hours)

Country calling code +1

Emergency number 911

Population 370,000 (1.3 million metro)

ELECTRICITY

Electricity 130V/60Hz

Type A 120V/60Hz

Type B 120V/60Hz

Good to Know

The water is usually safe to drink, but check NOLA Ready *(@nolaready)* for boil advisories.

Public Holidays

Note that when national holidays fall on a weekend, they are often celebrated on the nearest Friday or Monday so that everyone enjoys a three-day weekend. The following are all national holidays:

New Year's Day January 1

Martin Luther King Jr Day Third Monday in January

Presidents' Day Third Monday in February

Memorial Day Last Monday in May

Juneteenth June 19

Independence Day July 4

Labor Day First Monday in September

Indigenous People's Day (aka Columbus Day) Second Monday in October

Veterans Day November 11

Thanksgiving Fourth Thursday in November

Christmas Day December 25

Index

Experiences p000   Map pages **p000**

See also separate subindexes for:
Eating p166
Drinking p167
Shopping p167

INDEX

Eating

Drinking

Shopping

Send Us Your Feedback

We love to hear from travellers – your comments help make our books better. We read every word, and we guarantee that your feedback goes straight to the authors. Visit lonelyplanet.com/contact to submit your updates and suggestions.

Note: We may edit, reproduce and incorporate your comments in Lonely Planet products such as guidebooks, websites and digital products, so let us know if you are happy to have your name acknowledged. For a copy of our privacy policy visit lonelyplanet.com/legal.

Acknowledgements

Cover photograph: Saxophonist and paddle steamer. Siegfried Layda/Getty Images

Back photograph: City Park. EB Adventure Photography/Shutterstock

THIS BOOK

Destination Editor
Caroline Trefler

Production Editor
Megan Graieg

Cartographer
Anita Banh

Book Designer
Hannah Blackie

Assisting Editors
Shauna Daly

Cover Researcher
Marc Backwell

Thanks to
Ronan Abayawickrema, Joel Balsam , Karen Henderson, Adam Karlin, Alison Killilea, Amy Lysen, Doc O'Connell, Charlotte Orr

Paper in this book is certified against the Forest Stewardship Council™ standards. FSC™ promotes environmentally responsible, socially beneficial and economically viable management of the world's forests.

Published by Lonely Planet Global Limited
CRN 554153
5th edition – Aug 2025
ISBN 978 1 83758 488 8

10 9 8 7 6 5 4 3 2 1
Printed in Malaysia